Beautiful American Homes

Aside from the tepee, very little architecture in America is truly American in origin. Even the storied log cabin has its roots in Scandinavia. So it is with most of the architecture our ancestors brought over from England, Italy, Japan, Spain, France, and so many other countries. We take the best these countries have to give and put our own unique American spin on it.

A wealth of architects and designers working across the country cull the best of design standards and traditions from centuries of beautiful buildings and combine those rich details with all the modern amenities today's discriminating homeowner requires.

Here at Garlinghouse, we've been in the home plan business since 1907, so we know a thing or two about building trends and what homebuyers find appealing. We have designers and draftsmen who make modifications to plans and review blueprints when design firms submit them. We also have art, editorial, and customer service staff who look at plans all day long and who talk with customers like you about plans all day long. Each plan in this book has been carefully hand-selected, based not just upon sales, but also upon customer feedback, the considered opinions of our home design experts, and input from everyone on the Garlinghouse team.

If by chance you don't find what you're looking for in this book, please visit us at www.familyhomeplans.com, where you can search through thousands of plans on-line and find valuable information, advice, and resources on building your new home.

Plan 32358, page 86.

Plan 32316, page 16.

Plan 97313, page 148.

Plan 32109, page 37.

Beautiful American Homes

AN ACTIVE INTEREST MEDIA
PUBLICATION

GARLINGHOUSE, LLC

General Manager & Publisher	Marie L. Galastro
Art Director	Christopher Berrien
Managing Editor	Debra Cochran
Art Production Manager	Debra Novitch
Production Artist	Cindy King

For Plan Orders in United States
4125 Lafayette Center Drive, Suite 100
Chantilly, VA 20151
1-800-235-5700
For Plan Orders in Canada
The Garlinghouse Company
102 Ellis Street, Penticton, BC V2A 4L5
1-800-361-7526

ISBN 1-893536-17-3

LIBRARY OF CONGRESS 2004108402

728,37

CONTENTS

ABOVE: Our cover plan, number 96603, a French-country inspired cottage, is featured on page 158. Photography provided by Larry E. Belk Designs, Inc.

RESOURCES

Avoiding Common Problems with Your Builder

Seasoned Advice to Help Smooth the Construction Process

Building a house is a lot of work for the builder, but it's also a lot of work for the homeowner.

The homeowner's work begins with hiring the builder, or general contractor, which is where many projects start to go wrong. Yet, problems arise even with the best builders. Costly mistakes, lack of communication, poorly thought-out decisions, inadequate planning, failure to pay attention to the details, and inattention to budget can plague the best-intentioned home construction project.

Building a home is a complex process and a number of small mistakes will happen. On the other hand, you can avoid the biggest and costliest mistakes if you do your homework, communicate clearly, and respect the people building your home.

Avoiding the Low-Bid Dilemma

When you bid out your new home to a carefully selected list of contractors, it's awfully tempting to simply go with the lowest bid. That can be a mistake.

Massachusetts general contractor, Andrew Goldstein, calls low bids "seductive," and said it's a fallacy to assume that you should "put out the bid to three or four people and then go with the low bid. The problem with all bids is comparing them once they're in. If you really trace down the nightmares, you'll find that a large part of the problem is that people go for the low-bid price."

"When somebody bids something too low, they may have done it on purpose and plan to make it up later, or they may have done it accidentally. Either way, they'll soon be in trouble because they're losing money. On some level, they may start doing things

subconsciously like shaving time and cutting corners."

It's difficult for the average homeowner to know whether the low bid is really the lowest because all builders figure costs differently. "You have to get apples-to-apples bids, which is hard to do," Goldstein said. "Every builder does it differently. If you are going to put out bids, it's good to put out your own template."

Creating your own template means putting together a list of specific tasks that each contractor will have to treat similarly. "One way of creating a template is to take a look at your house. You probably won't be able to think of everything, but list things like painting, heating, foundation, roofing, framing, insulation, siding, electrical, plumbing, drywall, flooring, maybe tile. If a homeowner thinks about it for a half hour they can create this template. Say they even left out six or seven things—whatever they came up with at least gives them some basis to compare bids."

You might take this process a bit further and add more specifics to each category. For painting, ask for costs to apply two coats of a specific brand of paint; for plumbing, ask for total costs to rough-in, connect to the municipal water supply and sewerage system, and to install all fixtures, specifying the brands and models.

Once you receive quotes from your list of potential contractors, you can do equal comparisons. You still won't know everything, but you'll have a fair understanding of each builder's costs in relation to the others.

In other words, do your homework. "You have to do your homework or else don't complain," Goldstein said. "If you do it in a casual way, you should expect poor results."

Don't Forget the Paperwork

Let's assume that you chose a reputable, reliable builder, somebody you feel you can trust to do his best building your new home. Are your worries now over?

"Something you want to do now is protect yourself," Goldstein said. "Once you get a contract, make sure the builder has a license. And you should make sure they're carrying liability and workman's compensation insurance."

In most states, the homeowner will be liable for any damages or injuries occurring on the job if the

contractor isn't insured or is under-insured. Goldstein recommends that homeowners get certificates of insurance on both liability and workman's compensation, as well as on the builder's automobile insurance policy.

To further protect yourself, ask the builder for a lien waiver, which releases you from responsibility if the builder fails to pay subcontractors and suppliers.

"I can't speak for every state, but in Massachusetts, if you pay your builder and he does not pay his subcontractors, they can come after you. The same goes for the suppliers. You want to do as much as possible to make sure that once you pay him, he pays them."

The lien waiver is important for a number of reasons. Your contractor will have subcontracts with a lot of different companies and people, including roofers, excavators, mechanical contractors, painters,

"To protect yourself, ask the builder for a lien waver."

like laminate for a higher quality material like solid-surfacing. Minor changes usually don't cause problems. It's the bigger changes that cause problems because they have a ripple effect throughout the tightly scheduled construction project.

"If you assume the builder is competent and honest, the biggest problem in terms of budget and schedule is changes," Goldstein said. "If a homeowner cares about his money and his schedule, he should try to understand what he's building before he starts and be happy with it. But once you start changing your mind, it's costing you money and you're de-moralizing the builder."

Goldstein, whose general contracting company, Thought-forms Corporation, was chosen Custom Builder of the Year by *Custom Home* magazine, has thought a lot about this issue and offers good advice. "Change orders make the (construction) process less-efficient and cost more," he said. "Let's say he (the builder) has ordered the lights you chose for the kitchen but you say, 'No, we're going to get different lights.' Or he's ordered your cabinets and you've suddenly changed your mind. These changes add layers and layers of inefficiency," Goldstein said. "It's demoralizing to the builder and it sets a tone."

He gives a similar example involving decision making. "Let's say (the builder) bid the job with a tile allowance" and it's time to schedule the tile installer, "but you haven't picked out your tile yet," he said. "That can slow down a number of other jobs the builder has to schedule. What you're saying is that you've changed your mind, that the sub (contractor) doesn't have to come now. That sends a message to everybody on the job that the schedule isn't important."

and all the other trades that most contractors hire for a job. The contractor also buys materials from several different supply firms, where he likely has accounts. If they're not paid, every subcontractor and every supplier will have a right to file a "mechanic's lien" against your property if you're not protected by a lien waiver.

If such a lien is filed against your property, you can't sell or refinance the property until the lien is removed. Be wary of a builder who won't supply lien waivers.

Be Sparing with Changes

If we were to create a list of the biggest potential problems homeowners face when having a home built, change orders would probably rank right up there with hiring the builder.

A change order is a written order to the builder to change the plan of work, whether deleting some element of the construction project, adding some element, or, most likely, simply changing some element, such as swapping a lower-quality countertop material

"The biggest problem in terms of budget and schedule is changes."

Order on-line at www.familyhomeplans.com

A Few Fine Points

Take care of the little things and the big things take care of themselves, the saying goes. That being the case, the little things often add up to big things, and there are a few of the little things you should remember as you work with your contractor to build your home.

One of these is communication. "You should have formal meetings, even if you plan to show up every day," Goldstein said. "You should have a formal meeting scheduled. You sit down, you go over the issues, problems, questions. If there's a lot discussed, meeting notes are taken."

These don't all have to be long or in-depth meetings, but these meetings need to be established in a formal way. "What this means is that you're imposing a discipline, that there's a formal structure here," Goldstein said. "This doesn't limit you from having informal conversations. But it gives the meetings, and what you say at them, a little more weight."

These meetings will also help make sure you know what's going on so you're not taken by surprise.

"You're dealing with a construction project that is completely reliant on the people doing it," he said. "Other consumer products are made over and over, identically. Here we're doing it outdoors, it's a big thing, it costs a lot of money," and both the homeowner and builder will find the process smoother when things get talked out on a regular basis.

Finally, Goldstein offers a more subtle piece of advice, one whose meaning bears on virtually every relationship in the working world.

"I would suggest that, as much as possible, the homeowner should convey to the people who are working on their project—and I don't mean in a phony way or that they buy them things—but they should convey an appreciation that these people are trying to do a good job for them," he said. "These are people who are out there working with their hands, and this means a lot to them. If the homeowner comes across as arrogant, they'll ultimately end up with a worse job. But if, in an honest way, they can let it be known they appreciate that, they'll get a better job."

At Garlinghouse, you're buying more than a set of plans.

You're buying a history of exceptional customer service and understanding.

In addition to our experienced staff of sales professionals, The Garlinghouse Company maintains an expert staff of trained house design professionals to help guide you through the complex process of customizing your plans to meet all your needs and expectations.

We don't just want to sell you a plan, we want to partner with you in building your dream home. Some of the many services we offer our customers include:

Answers to Your Questions
If you have technical questions on any plan we sell, give us a call toll-free at 1-800-235-5700.

Customizing Your Stock Plan
Any plan we sell can be modified to become your custom home. For more information, see page 202.

Information for Budgeting Your New Home's Construction
A very general cost of building your new home can be arrived at using the so-called National Average Cost to Build, which is $110 per square foot. Based on that average, a 2,400-square-foot home would cost $264,000, including labor and materials, but excluding land, site preparation, windows, doors, cabinets, appliances, etc.

For a more inclusive rough estimate, Garlinghouse offers a Zip Quote estimate for every plan we sell. Based on current prices in your zip code area, we can provide a rough estimate of material and labor costs for the plans you select. See page 203 to learn more.

However, for a more accurate estimate of what it will cost to build your new home, we offer a full materials list, which lists the quantities, dimensions, and specifications for the major materials needed to build your home including appliances. Available at a modest additional charge, the materials list will allow you to get faster, more accurate bids from your contractors and building suppliers—and help you avoid paying for unused materials and waste. Due to differences in regional requirements and homeowner or builder preferences, electrical, plumbing, and heating/air conditioning equipment specifications are not designed specifically for each plan. See page 204 for additional information.

Garlinghouse blueprints have helped create a nation of homeowners, beginning back in 1907. Over the past century, we've made keeping up with the latest trends in floor plan design for new house construction our business. We understand the business of home plans and the real needs and expectations of the home plan buyer. To contact us, call 1-800-235-5700, or visit us on the web at www.familyhomeplans.com.

the
Garlinghouse
company

For America's best home plans.
Trust, value, and experience. Since 1907.

Colonial

The term Colonial originally referred to a time period in architecture rather than a specific style. The early colonists brought to America the prevailing architectural styles of their native countries. The French, Dutch, Spanish, and English settlers all brought with them tastes and preferences in style formed by their own cultural identities. That is why such seemingly disparate styles as Georgian and Spanish Colonial come under the general heading of Colonial Architecture.

In the late 1880s, a renewed interest in early English and Dutch houses led to the Colonial Revival style still popular today. The stately and symmetrical Georgian and Adam styles prevail in Colonial Revival, but there are still many fine examples of Dutch and French Colonial-inspired homes being designed today. A number of the homes in our "Southern" section were inspired by French Colonial prototypes.

Made for
Real Life

With three levels and an emphasis on open spaces and storage, this home packs a lot of living into just over 1,600 square feet. One large area combines the window-lined dining and family areas, as opposed to the more formal tradition of isolated eating areas. The kitchen, which is lined with counters, has a peninsula counter to divide the spaces. A cozy secondary bedroom and a separate den round out the 1,022-square-foot first floor.

The entire 580-square-foot second floor is dedicated to the master suite. Storage space surrounds the bedroom, including built-in cedar cabinets, which are located in the exterior kneewalls. The master bath includes a window-lined soaking tub and separate shower.

The lower floor was created for utility. The large two-car garage has additional space for storage or a workshop. The laundry is conveniently and discretely located at the bottom of the stairs. Another large room serves as a mechanical/storage area. This home is designed with a basement foundation.

ABOVE LEFT: A soaring central gable on a basic cape-style exterior adds height to this classic home. Heavy trim and a recessed entry with sidelights and transom give this colonial cottage added charm and detail.

ABOVE RIGHT: Sidelights and a transom surrounding a French door make the entry to this lovely cottage bright and inviting. Natural wood used on the floor and for the stair details combined with white paint make the small space seem more spacious.

BELOW: The side elevation shows the small windows that flank the chimney in the main living and dining area. The cape has long been an American favorite due to its practical versatility. This 21st-century update offers a lot of living space within its modest footprint.

Order on-line at www.familyhomeplans.com

ABOVE: The large combination family and dining room is flooded with natural light from three sides.

BELOW: A two-tier peninsula separates the kitchen and dining area providing extra counter space and a perfect spot to share a quick meal.

Plan Number 32385

Price Code	B
Total Finished	1,602 sq. ft.
First Finished	1,022 sq. ft.
Second Finished	580 sq. ft.
Basement Unfinished	473 sq. ft.
Garage Unfinished	547 sq. ft.
Dimensions	42'x28'
Foundation	Basement
Bedrooms	2
Full Baths	2

SECOND FLOOR

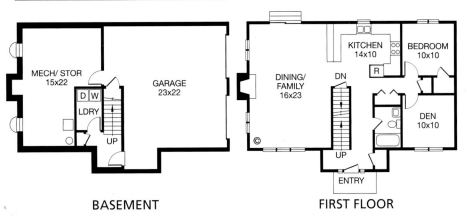

BASEMENT

FIRST FLOOR

Elegantly Relaxed
Colonial

A deep full-width front porch, with plenty of room for chairs, provides a warm welcome to this lovely mix of colonial styles. A formal living room and a dining room flank the center two-story hall. The big family room at the rear of the home is open to a polygonal breakfast area and the large, thoughtfully planned kitchen. To the right and front of the home are tucked the utility spaces with a large laundry room that includes a sink and a closet for drip-dry items. Also, here you'll find a powder room, kitchen pantry, and discrete access to the two-car garage. A secluded master bedroom, buffered from the rest of the activities of daily life by a deep walk-in closet and the master bath, lies at the back of the first floor. There are three additional bedrooms and three baths on the second floor, as well as bonus space for a future rec room and ample storage. This home is designed with a combination basement/crawlspace foundation.

ABOVE: The juxtapositioning of casual shingle siding with elaborate colonial details such as the Palladian window, classical columns, and front door with sidelights and elliptical fanlight creates an elegant yet relaxed facade.

BELOW: The open, winding staircase in the foyer rises over a convenient coat closet tucked into the asymmetrical arch.

ABOVE: A fine Adam-style mantel and fireplace surround with typical garland detail is a highlight of the generously proportioned living room.

RIGHT: The kitchen layout provides the best of both form and function with a bay window in the main work area, plenty of counter space, and a large center island. A nearby walk-in pantry provides additional storage.

Plan Number 57035

Price Code	Please call for pricing
Total Finished	3,170 sq. ft.
First Finished	2,086 sq. ft.
Second Finished	1,094 sq. ft.
Bonus Unfinished	372 sq. ft.
Dimensions	64'4"x61'10"
Foundation	Combo Basement/ Crawlspace
Bedrooms	4
Full Baths	2
3/4 Baths	2
Half Baths	1

FIRST FLOOR

© William E. Poole Architects, Inc.

SECOND FLOOR

Life of
Luxury

The classic good looks

of this two-story home are accented by the Palladian window over the entrance and Adam-style window surrounds using a keystone lintel above and paneled shutters to the sides. The formal spaces at the front of the home—a foyer flanked by a living room and a dining room—are open yet remain visually distinct through the use of varying ceiling treatments and columns. For family convenience the stairs are located with access directly into the kitchen and breakfast area. Windows located on either side of the corner sink flood the kitchen counter with natural light. The sunken family room with a fireplace brings a warm feeling to this private area of the house. On the second floor, a luxurious bedroom suite with double walk-in closets and a sloped ceiling is the highlight of this four bedroom plan. A balcony overlooking the foyer, a plant shelf, an arched window, a skylight, and a laundry chute are extra features that add style and value. This home is designed with a basement foundation.

Plan Number 92623	
Price Code	F
Total Finished	2,653 sq. ft.
First Finished	1,365 sq. ft.
Second Finished	1,288 sq. ft.
Basement Unfinished	1,217 sq. ft.
Garage Unfinished	491 sq. ft.
Dimensions	61'x37'6"
Foundation	Basement
Bedrooms	4
Full Baths	2
Half Baths	1

ABOVE: A Georgian facade, stately and symmetrical with a simple door surround, is embellished with a Palladian window and keystones over the first-floor windows.

SECOND FLOOR

FIRST FLOOR

Splendid
Saltbox

True to the origins of this classic style, a minimum of windows on the northern exposure helps conserve heat, while the rest of the home features enough windows to add warmth and light. A fireplace separates the living room from a gigantic great room that accesses the rear deck. The corner dining room, which lies beside the kitchen eating area, would make an ideal study. On the second floor, three bedrooms share space with a guest room that could also be used as a computer room. This home is designed with a basement foundation.

ABOVE: A classic saltbox-style exterior is wrapped around a great family floor plan.

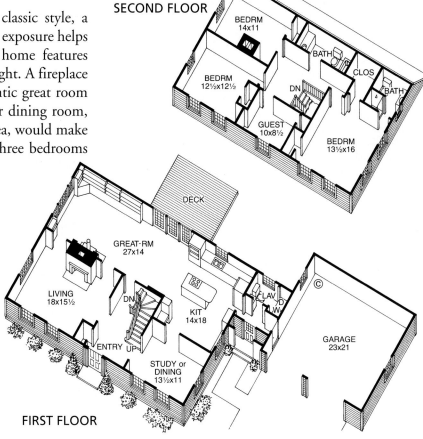

Plan Number 19476	
Price Code	E
Total Finished	2,405 sq. ft.
First Finished	1,340 sq. ft.
Second Finished	1,065 sq. ft.
Dimensions	74'x38'8"
Foundation	Basement
Bedrooms	4
Full Baths	1
3/4 Baths	1
Half Baths	1

Authentically
Colonial

On the outside, this saltbox may look like a perfect 18th-century structure, but, once built, it will have the advantage of 21st-century wiring and plumbing. Modern-day amenities include ample storage, a spacious master bath, and a three-car garage. The main entry opens to the home's formal rooms, with a living room to the left and a dining room on the right. Toward the rear are the more informal spaces. The keeping room features a fireplace on the interior wall, with triple windows on the opposite. There's also an informal entrance through the service area that connects the garage to the first floor. This area offers a closet, a half bath, and a laundry room conveniently located near a large kitchen pantry. Three spacious bedrooms and two generous full baths make up the second floor. The unfinished attic adds 988 square feet. This home is designed with a basement foundation.

ABOVE: The basic home style of our colonial ancestors is flawlessly recreated here in this 21st-century update of an early-American saltbox.

BELOW: The winding staircase in the entry provides the perfect location to hide a coat closet.

ABOVE: Clean lines of trim and molding highlighted with a simple color scheme and offset by the rich wood floor offer elegant simplicity in the living room and throughout the rest of the home.

LEFT: Antiques and modern period recreations mix to great effect in the dining room.

ABOVE: Trim and wood beams in the keeping room add period authenticity.

LEFT: The kitchen maintains a period look while incorporating all the modern amenities. An adjacent walk-in pantry located near the garage and side door is convenient for unloading groceries.

BELOW: The master bedroom, unlike its colonial precedents, includes a large bath with whirlpool tub and separate shower as well as a deep walk-in closet.

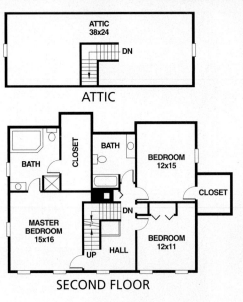

ATTIC
38x24

DN

ATTIC

CLOSET
BATH
BATH
BEDROOM
12x15
CLOSET
MASTER
BEDROOM
15x16
DN
UP   HALL
BEDROOM
12x11

SECOND FLOOR

PORCH
KEEPING
ROOM
14x18
KITCHEN
12x10
UP
AUDIO
ROOM
11x11
R
D
W
P
GARAGE
22x32
DN
LIVING
17x16
ENTRY
UP
DINING
12x13
PORCH

FIRST FLOOR

Plan Number 32316

Price Code	G
Total Finished	2,752 sq. ft.
First Finished	1,533 sq. ft.
Second Finished	1,219 sq. ft.
Attic Unfinished	988 sq. ft.
Garage Unfinished	828 sq. ft.
Dimensions	74'4"x37'6"
Foundation	Basement
Bedrooms	3
Full Baths	2
Half Baths	1

Modern Family
Perfection

A double-height porch makes quite a first impression in this spacious family home. A long living room to the left of the center entry and a formal dining room to the right give a nod to the classic floor plans of this home's architectural ancestors. Once you pass those rooms, this house is all modern. A kitchen with angled workspaces, center island, and eating bar opens to a bay-windowed eating nook overlooking a rear porch. The first-floor master suite features a sitting area, well-appointed bath, and deep walk-in closet. A utility room, storage space, and a three-car garage round out the first floor. On the second floor, three good size bedrooms and two full baths share space with a tv room. This home is designed with basement, crawlspace, and slab foundation options.

ABOVE: The balance and symmetry of this home's stately exterior opens up on the inside to reveal spacious, open rooms with interesting angles and lots of windows.

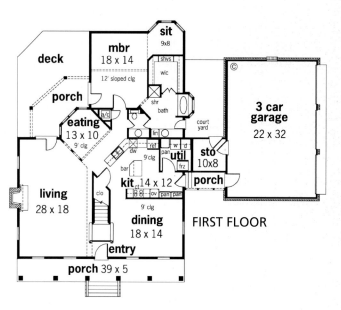

SECOND FLOOR

FIRST FLOOR

Plan Number 65662	
Price Code	G
Total Finished	2,888 sq. ft.
First Finished	1,768 sq. ft.
Second Finished	1,120 sq. ft.
Garage Unfinished	768 sq. ft.
Porch Unfinished	357 sq. ft.
Dimensions	72'x58'
Foundation	Basement
	Crawlspace
	Slab
Bedrooms	4
Full Baths	3

Proud **Tradition**

This traditional floor plan combines open and airy spaces tailored for today's way of life with detailing to match the home's traditional architectural style. On the first floor, the entry is flanked by formal dining and living rooms. A large family room, breakfast area, and kitchen make up the open, casual family spaces. The optional lower floor houses a two-car garage, guest room, generous media room, and full bath.

The second floor has a large master suite, which includes a sitting room with fireplace, dual walk-in closets, and a private bath. Three additional bedrooms share a full bath conveniently located next to a laundry room. This home is designed with a basement foundation.

ABOVE: A stately brick exterior with a prominent center gable gives this home the appeal of timeless quality.

Plan Number 32045	
Price Code	G
Total Finished	2,980 sq. ft.
First Finished	1,480 sq. ft.
Second Finished	1,500 sq. ft.
Lower Unfinished	760 sq. ft.
Garage Unfinished	720 sq. ft.
Dimensions	42'x41'
Foundation	Basement
Bedrooms	4
Full Baths	2
Half Baths	1

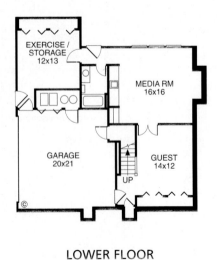

LOWER FLOOR

FIRST FLOOR

SECOND FLOOR

Order on-line at www.familyhomeplans.com

Photography: Mike Moreland

ABOVE: A symmetrically balanced entry with fan and sidelights, slender Doric columns supporting a gabled porch roof, and keystone lintels over the windows mark this stylish home as Colonial Revival.

Plan Number 32218	
Price Code	H
Total Finished	3,109 sq. ft.
First Finished	2,474 sq. ft.
Second Finished	635 sq. ft.
Basement Unfinished	2,474 sq. ft.
Garage Unfinished	792 sq. ft.
Dimensions	101'x61'
Foundation	Crawlspace
Bedrooms	4
Full Baths	3
Half Baths	1

Colonial **Revival**

Forget the conventional floor plan with a formal living room just inside the entry, this design offers a twist to the traditional by putting a guest room/study in its place. A large great room does double duty, providing space for formal and informal occasions. With a vaulted ceiling, a fireplace, and windows overlooking the backyard, this room is the home's centerpiece. The adjacent sunroom and roomy kitchen on the right side of the home lead to a secondary entrance, utility room, powder room, and three-car garage. The first floor master suite on the left side is a spacious retreat for the homeowner. Two more bedrooms, a full bath, and two big attic storage areas make up the second floor. This home is designed with a crawlspace foundation.

FIRST FLOOR

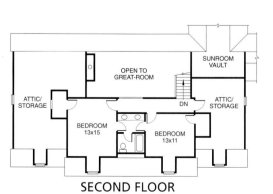

SECOND FLOOR

Photography: Courtesy of the Designer

Elegant
Brick Elevation

An elegant door surround and rows of shuttered windows lend timeless beauty to this home. A two-story entry hall opens to the formal dining and living room and views the magnificent great room. The spacious great room, with cathedral ceiling, has a fireplace flanked by floor to ceiling windows. The den is comfortable and secluded with French doors, bayed windows, and a wet bar. Amenities in the kitchen and bayed breakfast area include a built-in desk, wrapping counters and a popular island counter. The master suite has a luxurious dressing/bath area with a large walk-in closet. Upstairs each secondary bedroom has its own roomy closet and private bathroom. This home is designed with a basement foundation.

ABOVE: This impressive Colonial Revival features a wealth of rich trim moldings enhancing its elegant facade. A broken pediment crowning the door surround, a deep cornice with dentil molding, and built-up window caps add to the richness.

Plan Number 94994

Price Code	G
Total Finished	2,957 sq. ft.
First Finished	2,063 sq. ft.
Second Finished	894 sq. ft.
Basement Unfinished	2,063 sq. ft.
Garage Unfinished	666 sq. ft.
Dimensions	72'8"x51'4"
Foundation	Basement
Bedrooms	4
Full Baths	2
3/4 Baths	2
Half Baths	1

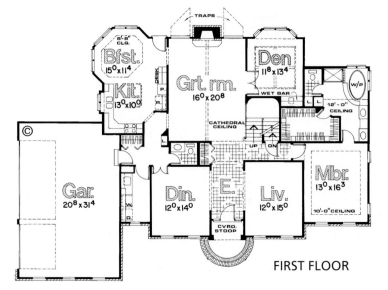

FIRST FLOOR

SECOND FLOOR

The Best of
Old and New

ABOVE: The exterior is modeled after the Colonial New England farmhouses of the early 1700s—even down to the additions that would have been added on to such a house over generations.

You might mistake this home for a genuine pre-Revolutionary Georgian dwelling, but modern-day amenities give it the best of both worlds. A center hall entry with winding staircase opens to the formal living room on one side and also leads straight through to the back of the home. A formal dining room sits on the entry's other side, connecting to a kitchen with ample counter space and an eating bar. The kitchen also serves the sunken nook, which leads to a sprawling family room with its own fireplace and access to a long side porch. The second-floor master bedroom includes a sitting area, walk-in closet, and full bath. Three more bedrooms round out this floor. This home is designed with a basement foundation.

SECOND FLOOR

FIRST FLOOR

Plan Number 32079

Price Code	I
Total Finished	3,458 sq. ft.
First Finished	2,026 sq. ft.
Second Finished	1,432 sq. ft.
Basement Unfinished	2,030 sq. ft.
Garage Unfinished	841 sq. ft.
Dimensions	53'x100'6"
Foundation	Basement
Bedrooms	4
Full Baths	2
Half Baths	1

Grand
Greek Revival

ABOVE: Although this design lacks the typical front portico inspired by the Greek temples that served as the prototypes for American Greek Revival architecture, it does have a front-facing pedimented gable above a flat facade, tall windows, and an impressive doorway.

The street door of this charming house borrows a tradition from the famous Charleston single houses by opening onto a deep side porch rather than into the house itself. The side porch shades two sets of Palladian windows, which flank the entry. A gallery sits beside the entry, while pocket doors slide open to reveal a private library with a fireplace. A huge kitchen is strategically located between the formal dining room and a combination breakfast/family room, which has access to a screen porch on the side. A keeping room enjoys a fireplace of its own, while a spacious guest room sits right next door. Three secondary bedrooms and two full baths share one wing of the second floor. The master suite features double doors to a private, covered porch at one end and a fireplace, which shares a chimney with the library fireplace on the floor below, at the other end. The master bath connects to a room-sized walk-in closet that's right beside a laundry room conveniently located in the middle of the four second-floor bedrooms. This home is designed with a combination basement and crawlspace foundation.

FIRST FLOOR

SECOND FLOOR

Plan Number 32211	
Price Code	K
Total Finished	3,833 sq. ft.
First Finished	2,093 sq. ft.
Second Finished	1,740 sq. ft.
Dimensions	76'4"x67'
Foundation	Combination Basement/ Crawlspace
Bedrooms	5
Full Baths	4
Half Baths	2

ABOVE: Wooden pilasters surrounding a Georgian-style door rise up to visually support a centered roof pediment calling attention to the entry of this stunning colonial home.

BELOW: An elegant staircase, arched doorways, and a leaded glass fanlight over pocket doors leading to the family room create an impression of history and character in this new home.

Impressive
Appeal

A stately symmetrical

front facade sets the tone from the curb for this grand design. Once inside the elegant two-story foyer with its magnificently detailed staircase and trim, the quality found throughout the home is obvious. Formal rooms at the front of the home are surrounded by family spaces. To the rear is a long double-height family room while a storage laden kitchen/breakfast area to the right leads to a utility room and two-car garage. On the left, a master suite with his and her wardrobes sits next to a private study. Three additional bedrooms and a future rec room are on the spacious second floor. This home is designed with a combination basement and crawlspace foundation.

ABOVE: Tall windows in the living room open to the front of the home. Ten-foot ceilings throughout the first floor contribute to the sense of spacious elegance.

LEFT: Heavy crown molding and a chair rail add formality to the dining room.

BELOW: The casual and open breakfast area at the front of the kitchen is separated from the formal dining room by a butler's pantry providing the perfect place to store china and silver. A walk-in pantry provides additional convenience.

LEFT: A big Palladian window in the master bedroom brightens a sitting area.

BELOW: The rear elevation of the home is enlivened by the impressive arrangement of windows for the family room.

Plan Number 57055

Price Code	Please call for pricing
Total Finished	4,204 sq. ft.
First Finished	2,988 sq. ft.
Second Finished	1,216 sq. ft.
Basement Unfinished	2,988 sq. ft.
Bonus Unfinished	485 sq. ft.
Dimensions	83'x70'
Foundation	Basement
Bedrooms	4
Full Baths	3
3/4 Baths	1
Half Baths	2

FIRST FLOOR

SECOND FLOOR

ABOVE: A deep front porch with plenty of room for comfortable chairs is a welcome and attractive addition to any home.

LEFT: A gracefully proportioned gambrel roof with flared, overhanging eaves is a hallmark of American Dutch colonial style. The gambrel roof form developed as a means of increasing useable attic space.

BELOW: Ionic columns with exaggerated capitals support the arched entrance to the dining room.

Hudson Valley
Dutch Colonial

The exterior of this home maintains a lovely period charm while the interior strikes a balance between the best of old and new. The use of exposed beams, heavy molding, and classical columns give the interior a vintage air belied by the modern amenities found throughout. At the front of the home, the formal spaces balance the foyer. Beyond the foyer lies the great room where a vaulted ceiling with exposed beams rises over a large stone hearth. Open to this space is the breakfast area and kitchen where the custom colonial look of the cabinetry offsets the modern stainless steel appliances. A master suite completes the first floor. Three additional bedrooms share the second floor with ample storage and bonus space. This home is designed with a crawlspace foundation.

ABOVE: A great stone hearth in the family room mimics the stone facing found on the exterior of the home.

RIGHT: Colonial style of the built-in, custom-look cabinets meets 21st century sleek of the high-end stainless steel appliances in the kitchen. The mix of texture and style—rough-hewn beams and custom-crafted cabinetry alongside shimmering, high-tech stainless—balances beautifully creating a room that is both comfortable and functional.

BELOW: The rear elevation of the home is as authentically detailed as the front and just as attractive.

Plan Number 57043

Price Code	Please call for pricing
Total Finished	4,299 sq. ft.
First Finished	3,016 sq. ft.
Second Finished	1,283 sq. ft.
Bonus Unfinished	757 sq. ft.
Dimensions	105'x69'
Foundation	Crawlspace
Bedrooms	5
Full Baths	5
Half Baths	2

FIRST FLOOR

SECOND FLOOR

Historic Charm,
Stately
Elegance

The grand entry sets the stage for the fine details and craftsmanship found throughout this classic design. Arches lead the way to the formal dining and living rooms that flank the entrance. French doors open into the library, where a warm and inviting atmosphere is enhanced by a fireplace, one of the home's three. The living and family rooms contain the two other fireplaces. The breakfast area is open to the kitchen, which is filled with work space. Doors lead out from both the family room and the library to the rear patio. A mudroom and home office round out the 2,561-square-foot first floor. The secondary bedrooms share the 2,012-square-foot second floor with the impressive master suite. The suite features its own sitting room, walk-in closet, and five-piece bath. The master suite also has access to a private deck and storage room. This home is designed with a basement foundation.

ABOVE: A quartet of dormers, a mix of stone and clapboard facing, telescoping rooflines, and an elegant Adam-style portico entry provide this facade with a stately elegance reminiscent of fine 18th century architecture.

BELOW: The foyer shows off the range of fine architectural elements found throughout, from the upper-level bridge and loft, to the hardwood flooring, to the arched entry at the rear of the foyer.

Photography: Craig Dugan, Hedrich-Blessing

ABOVE: Built-in cabinets and shelves in the living room are a testament to fine craftsmanship. The doorway to the right leads through French doors to the library.

LEFT: Seen from the arched entry, windows flank an elegant fireplace surround embellished with Adam-style appliques in the living room, creating the perfect balance of light and warmth.

BELOW LEFT: Rich paneling and heavy trim moldings in the library create a plush sanctuary crowned by a decorative ceiling. The large room opens onto a rear patio.

BELOW: The formal dining room is set apart from the rest of the rooms, yet through careful design remains open and easily accessible to the entry, breakfast room, and, most importantly, the kitchen.

ABOVE, LEFT AND RIGHT: In the family room (LEFT), a box-beam ceiling is a lovely complement to the fireplace and built-ins. The breakfast room (RIGHT) is tied to the family room and the kitchen by the same wall color and beam ceiling treatment.

RIGHT: Custom cabinetry in the kitchen adds to the beauty and efficiency of the sunny space.

BELOW: Built-in lockers in the mudroom just inside the family entrance help keep the living spaces clear of clutter.

Plan Number 32425

Price Code	L
Total Finished	4,573 sq. ft.
First Finished	2,561 sq. ft.
Second Finished	2,012 sq. ft.
Basement Unfinished	2,522 sq. ft.
Deck Unfinished	73 sq. ft.
Dimensions	68'x54'3"
Foundation	Basement
Bedrooms	4
Full Baths	3
Half Baths	2

ABOVE: The spacious master bath features plenty of room for a large corner tub surrounded by windows.

ABOVE LEFT: French doors lead from the master bedroom onto a private deck. The homeowner added another window (to the right of the bed) to add more light.

LEFT: The homeowner chose to warm up the master suite's sitting room with the addition of a gas fireplace.

FIRST FLOOR

SECOND FLOOR

Craftsman

The Craftsman style dominated the first two decades of the twentieth century. One of the first truly American styles of architecture, Craftsman homes introduced a more open floor plan, supplanting earlier Victorian and Colonial styles in popularity. Low-pitched roofs, usually gabled, with wide eave overhangs and exposed roof rafters combined with a rich variety of natural materials are hallmarks of this popular style.

Common to the Craftsman-style home is the outdoor room. Every period example has at least one porch, if not several, and often includes a pergola as well. The outdoor room is still a feature homeowners prize today as is amply demonstrated in the fine 21st century Craftsman adaptations we've collected on the following pages.

Cozy
Bungalow

Craftsman-style details enliven the exterior of this charming home, from the square, tapered porch supports to the prominent decorative brace under the front gable. A formal dining room at the front of the home is separated from the entry by half walls. Behind the dining room, a counter-lined kitchen features a serving bar that curves out into the large living room at the rear of the home. The first floor master suite is nestled into the front projecting gable ensuring privacy. Two more bedrooms on the second floor share a full bath that's compartmentalized for convenient shared use. This home is designed with a crawlspace foundation.

ABOVE: Gently sloping gables with wide overhangs, bands of grouped windows, and a shady, inviting porch give Craftsman flair to this perfect bungalow.

SECOND FLOOR

Plan Number 32088	
Price Code	B
Total Finished	1,654 sq. ft.
First Finished	1,096 sq. ft.
Second Finished	558 sq. ft.
Garage Unfinished	520 sq. ft.
Porch Unfinished	144 sq. ft.
Dimensions	62'x44'
Foundation	Crawlspace
Bedrooms	3
Full Baths	1
3/4 Baths	1
Half Baths	1

FIRST FLOOR

ABOVE: Columns support the covered porch, which provides space for fair-weather entertaining.

Photography: Courtesy of the Designer

SECOND FLOOR

BED 3
10²×11²

BED 2
10²×11²

COMPUTER
LOFT

OPEN

FIRST FLOOR

MORN.
10²×10²

KITCH.
9²×10²

MASTER
10²×14²

10²×16.

GREAT
ROOM
13²×20²
12² CLG.

PANT

GARAGE
21²×21²

COVERED
PORCH

Tradition
With a Twist

A traditional Craftsman-style exterior holds convenient modern spaces in this handsome home. Wide counters nearly encircle the kitchen, which lies adjacent to a morning room. Off to the side, you'll find a fireplace-warmed great room. The first-floor master suite occupies its own corner, complete with a decorative ceiling and a private full bath. A second-floor computer loft overlooks the entry, providing the ideal spot for either work, study, or play. Two comfortable bedrooms in the rear have access to their own full bath. This home is designed with a basement foundation. Alternate foundation options available at an additional charge. Please call 1-800-235-5700 for more information.

Plan Number 68116

Price Code	C
Total Finished	1,818 sq. ft.
First Finished	1,302 sq. ft.
Second Finished	516 sq. ft.
Basement Unfinished	1,302 sq. ft.
Garage Unfinished	475 sq. ft.
Dimensions	50'x48'
Foundation	Basement
Bedrooms	3
Full Baths	2
Half Baths	1

Photography: James Yochum Photography

Decked Out

Shapes and angles are carefully planned in this striking design to take advantage of the surrounding views. Hundreds of square feet of covered porch and open deck make it a nature lover's delight. A sense of openness suffuses the 1,213 square-foot first floor. The dining room and kitchen are in a separate wing of the house while remaining visually open to the first floor through the screen porch. The octagonal living room rises up two stories surrounded by walls of windows. The master suite enjoys its own private corner on the first floor, separated from the two upstairs bedrooms. This home is designed with a basement foundation.

ABOVE: This home is angled to catch light at every turn, with an ample supply of windows, including the clerestory above the entry.

BELOW: The deep overhang of the roof, typical of Craftsman-style homes, shades the soaring two-story living room from direct sun even as banks of windows across the rear of the home draw in the light.

ABOVE: The soaring living room is the center of this home, with all other spaces designed in relation to this one fantastic room.

RIGHT: The two-story living room draws visitors in from the entry. Even the stairwell is brightly lit with natural light thanks to thoughtfully placed windows.

BELOW: Two sets of triple transom-topped windows open the first floor master bedroom up to the home's lovely wooded site.

ABOVE & RIGHT: This homeowner modified the plan to enclose the screen porch for use as a dining room (RIGHT). This freed up the space reserved for the dining room on the original floor plan for use as a family room (ABOVE) that's open to the kitchen, creating a large, casual family space secluded to one side of the home.

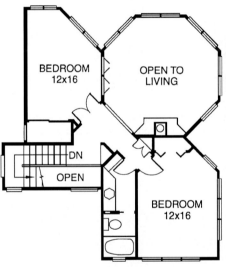

SECOND FLOOR

BEDROOM 12x16

OPEN TO LIVING

DN

OPEN

BEDROOM 12x16

Plan Number 32109

Price Code	D
Total Finished	2,038 sq. ft.
First Finished	1,213 sq. ft.
Second Finished	825 sq. ft.
Basement Unfinished	1,213 sq. ft.
Deck Unfinished	535 sq. ft.
Porch Unfinished	144 sq. ft.
Dimensions	46'4"x37'8"
Foundation	Basement
Bedrooms	3
Full Baths	1
3/4 Baths	1
Half Baths	1

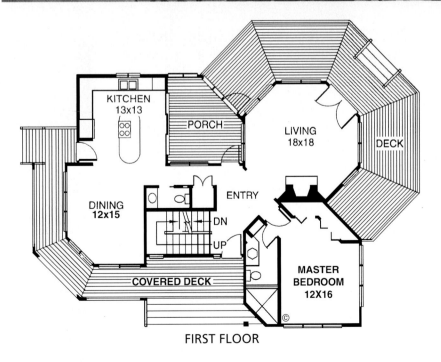

KITCHEN 13x13

PORCH

LIVING 18x18

DECK

DINING 12x15

ENTRY

DN

UP

MASTER BEDROOM 12X16

COVERED DECK

FIRST FLOOR

Traditional
Details

ABOVE: Clapboard and cedar-shake siding, front facing gables, exposed eave brackets, and square tapered porch supports establish timeless appeal.

BELOW: Half walls and columns provide an elegant yet simple frame for the entry to the living room.

Sometimes it's the simple details

that make the biggest statement. Such is the case with this house, whose gable roofline, cedar-shake siding accents, and simple front porch columns showcase the classic details of traditional design. The garage in the back makes the home suitable for neighborhoods with narrow lots and alley access. The living and dining rooms flank the entry, both providing views to the front. The kitchen features an island with a cooktop and ample pantry storage beneath the U-shape staircase. The second-floor master suite includes a tub, shower, dual-sink vanity, and a walk-in closet. Two additional bedrooms share a full bath. The first floor has 1,211 square feet and the second floor has 867 square feet. This home is designed with a crawlspace foundation.

Order on-line at www.familyhomeplans.com

Plan Number 32049

Price Code	D
Total Finished	2,078 sq. ft.
First Finished	1,211 sq. ft.
Second Finished	867 sq. ft.
Dimensions	40'6"x65'
Foundation	Crawlspace
Bedrooms	3
Full Baths	2
Half Baths	1

LEFT: The entry to the formal dining room is a mirror image of its living room counterpart.

BELOW: A large window combined with light cabinetry brighten the kitchen. Just beyond the breakfast nook to the left is the door to the laundry room and garage. A gas fireplace serves as a practical and attractive room divider between the kitchen area and the family room

SECOND FLOOR

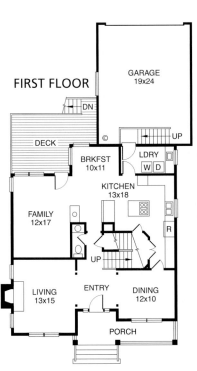

FIRST FLOOR

Stylish Family
Home

The appealing entry, sheltered within a small porch, leads into a cozy living room offering a quiet retreat at the front of the home. A wide stair hall leads to the rear of the home, opening up with dramatic impact to a large, combination great room—dining room—kitchen space visually separated by varying ceiling heights. The second floor features a sumptuous master suite including plans for a double-sided gas fireplace to be shared by the sitting area and the large whirlpool tub in the master bath. Two secondary bedrooms, a full hall bath, and a convenient laundry room are also on the second floor. The lower level includes a fourth bedroom and large recreation room. This home is designed with a basement foundation.

ABOVE: The hipped roof and low vertical lines of Prairie style are married to Craftsman-inspired details such as exposed roof beams and rafter tails in this stylish family home.

BELOW: The secluded living room offers a quiet retreat and introduces the Craftsman-style decor that is prevalent throughout the rest of the home.

ABOVE: Abundant workspace and attractive cabinetry are highlights of the kitchen. An octagonal dining area creates an intimate space within the larger great room.

RIGHT: Craftsman-inspired details in the fireplace surround lend authenticity to the open, comfortable area of the great room.

Plan Number 50067

Price Code	F
Total Finished	2,691 sq. ft.
First Finished	1,160 sq. ft.
Second Finished	1,531 sq. ft.
Basement Unfinished	1,160 sq. ft.
Garage Unfinished	465 sq. ft.
Deck Unfinished	339 sq. ft.
Porch Unfinished	75 sq. ft.
Dimensions	37'8"x53'
Foundation	Basement
Bedrooms	3
Full Baths	2
Half Baths	1

BASEMENT

FIRST FLOOR

SECOND FLOOR

Photography: Courtesy of the Designer

Plenty of **Room**

This Craftsman-style home offers everything from an abundance of light to a plethora of storage space. The first floor holds the common areas, each separated by function. The entry opens on the right to a private study and on the left to the formal living room. That room blends into the dining area, separated by a pair of columns. The family room is located in the right wing, sharing space with the breakfast nook and counter-lined kitchen.

Three bedrooms and 468 square feet of bonus space fill the second floor. Each bedroom features generous closet space and one secondary bedroom accesses its own private bath. The other secondary bedroom is just a step away from a full bath. The master suite wraps around the floor and connects to a big attic storage space. The laundry room is conveniently located in the center of the bedrooms. An extra bay in the garage can house a third vehicle or be used for a workshop or additional storage space. This home is designed with a crawlspace foundation.

ABOVE: This home presents architectural interest from every angle, from the square porch supports on stone bases to the trio of gables, contrasting siding, and bump-out window. A low roof line and decorative support brackets are typical of Craftsman style homes.

BELOW LEFT: The counter-lined kitchen features a big center island and walk-in pantry. The corner of windows floods the work space with natural light.

BELOW: The kitchen is open to the breakfast nook, which offers access to a covered porch at the rear of the home.

Order on-line at www.familyhomeplans.com

ABOVE: Separated from the entry with half walls, soffits, and columns, the formal living room with fireplace is a welcome and inviting sight for guests and family members. Two double-hung windows flanking a fixed picture-window at the front of the room look out over the deep front porch. To the right, you can see the opening to the dining room.

LEFT: In the dining room, a bump-out creates the perfect alcove for a side board, easing traffic patterns around the dining table and through to the kitchen. The size and scale of the windows in the alcove match those of the windows that flank the fireplace in the living room. The rear wall of the dining room also contains a matching set of windows to those at the front of the living room providing continuity on the interior as well as the exterior.

ABOVE: The family room presents a cozy and intimate feel despite its generous size. A tiled fireplace topped with a wooden television cabinet and mantel with arts and crafts detailing adds both style and convenience.

LEFT: At the head of the stairs, double doors lead into the master bedroom, which offers two corners of windows and an alcove that would make a charming sitting area or secluded reading spot.

RIGHT: The spacious master bath has plenty of room for a soaking tub, separate shower, dual vanity, dressing table, and toilet compartment. The room leads into a deep walk-in closet and a large attic storage space beyond that. Two additional full baths can be found on the second floor easing the morning rush.

Plan Number 32422

Price Code	G
Total Finished	2,873 sq. ft.
First Finished	1,525 sq. ft.
Second Finished	1,348 sq. ft.
Bonus Unfinished	468 sq. ft.
Garage Unfinished	738 sq. ft.
Deck Unfinished	162 sq. ft.
Porch Unfinished	222 sq. ft.
Dimensions	62'6"x54'
Foundation	Crawlspace
Bedrooms	3
Full Baths	3
Half Baths	1

*This home cannot be built in the state of Washington.

ABOVE: Windows line every elevation of the home, including a skylight, bringing the outdoors in, while a covered porch at the rear offers space to enjoy nicer days.

BELOW: A sunny alcove in a secondary bedroom makes a perfect window seat.

SECOND FLOOR

FIRST FLOOR

Photography: James Yochum Photography

Tradition in Detail

The warm personality of this home is reflected in dozens of thoughtful touches, from the kitchenette in the lower floor family room to built-in storage throughout the plan. The front porch, with tapered supports topping stone bases, shelters the multiple windows of the dining room and office/den, while allowing light to stream in. Once inside the entry, the living room sits straight ahead, with the open kitchen and breakfast area to the right. Behind this area, the mudroom affords not only a spacious rear entry, but also a comfortable window seat and closet-like paneled lockers for storage. The master suite completes the right wing of the main floor, while the secondary bedrooms sit below. With a vast family room, kitchenette, storage, and full baths, the lower floor could be a home of its own. This home is designed with a basement foundation.

ABOVE: A bungalow-style porch is topped by a central gable that fills the entry hall with light. Stonework accents the front porch, which shades the windows of the dining room and office/den.

BELOW: From the foyer, it's a short trip past the office/den to the stairs, which lead down into a sprawling family room.

ABOVE: Recessed built-ins surround the living room fireplace under a cathedral ceiling with exposed beams.

RIGHT: Wainscoting and built-ins add to the charm of the dining room.

BELOW: Updated Craftsman-style details—like this bookcase and column separating the den from the entry—fill the home.

ABOVE: Contrasting light and dark finishes open up the kitchen.

LEFT: A bench at the breakfast table keeps the room open, providing a clear view through the French doors.

RIGHT: Built-in lockers right inside the family entrance keep the rest of the house clear of discarded coats, shoes, book bags—all those things we use daily and never quite know where to keep.

LEFT: The decor of the master bedroom—dark gray-green walls, a dark oak stain Craftsman-style bed, wicker accent pieces—mirrors the view through the double set of double-hung windows.

BELOW LEFT: The tub in the master bath is tucked into a sunny niche. Brackets at the top echo the brackets found throughout the home, from the exterior eaves to the fireplace niche in the living room.

BELOW: Two small windows draw light into a vanity area in the master bath.

Plan Number 32439

Price Code	L
Total Finished	4,236 sq. ft.
Main Finished	2,118 sq. ft.
Lower Finished	2,118 sq. ft.
Garage Unfinished	842 sq. ft.
Deck Unfinished	196 sq. ft.
Porch Unfinished	454 sq. ft.
Dimensions	75'8½"x66'
Foundation	Basement
Bedrooms	4
Full Baths	2
3/4 Baths	1
Half Baths	1

MAIN FLOOR

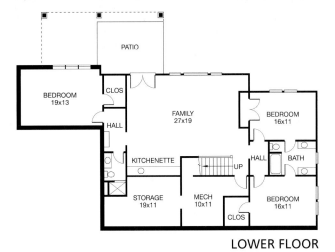

LOWER FLOOR

Forest **Cottage**

Living in the woods just got stylish. The exterior of this home exhilarates in the design elements of a storybook cottage, while the interior is all luxurious comfort. Rooms sprawl openly into each other on the first floor, with only the library/den and the screen porch set apart from the flow. The gourmet kitchen serves the dining area, snack bar, great room, and the window-lit breakfast area equally well. From nearly every space, large windows frame views of nature.

The organic forms and materials used in the design of this house help it to blend beautifully with its setting while the decks, screen porch, and breezeway offer ample opportunity to blend lifestyle to surroundings. A large, curving deck off the great room and screen porch wraps around the front of the home and connects to the breezeway. A separate deck is just outside the French doors of the dining room.

Three bedrooms and three full baths are upstairs, offering secluded privacy, in perfect juxtaposition to the open first floor. In the master bedroom, a large bump-out bath with whirlpool is set beneath a triple window. The two secondary bedrooms each have a private bath.

A lower floor provides an additional 1,230 square feet, including a guest room, media room, and a playroom among other things. This home is designed with a basement foundation.

ABOVE: The kitchen island contains the cooktop and dishwasher, as well as plenty of counter space and cabinets.

RIGHT: The other side of the island doubles as a desk area. An arched opening separates the kitchen from the great room.

BELOW: A sitting area across from the kitchen island is bathed in light from banks of transom-topped windows.

ABOVE: In the sunny breakfast nook off the kitchen, built-in seating and transom-topped windows outlined in cherry trim exemplify a Craftsman-style attention to detail found throughout the home.

LEFT: A built-in settee and cabinet are near the main entrance.

BELOW: A niche between the great room and kitchen serves as a coffee nook.

ABOVE: The rounded deck off the great room amplifies the shape of the window in the gable above. Decking wraps around much of the home's perimeter.

Plan Number 32063

Price Code	L
Total Finished	4,283 sq. ft.
First Finished	1,642 sq. ft.
Second Finished	1,411 sq. ft.
Lower Finished	1,230 sq. ft.
Basement Unfinished	412 sq. ft.
Deck Unfinished	207 sq. ft.
Porch Unfinished	1,000 sq. ft.
Dimensions	92'x61'
Foundation	Basement
Bedrooms	4
Full Baths	4
Half Baths	1

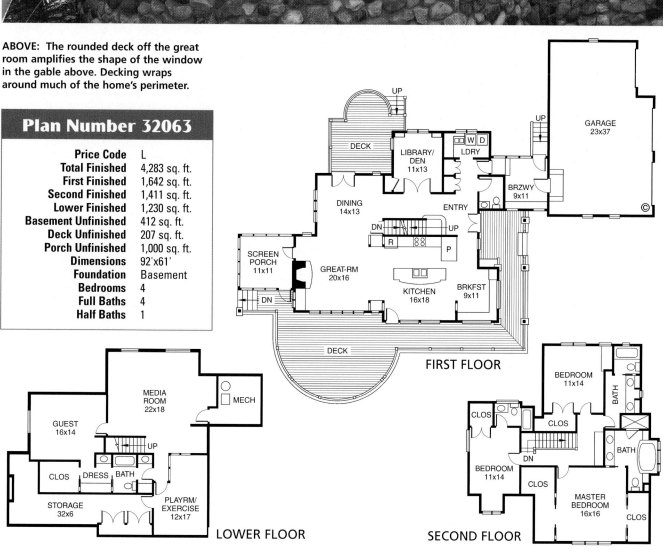

FIRST FLOOR

LOWER FLOOR

SECOND FLOOR

Photography courtesy of the designer

Cottage Revival

Gables, arches, and varied rooflines combined with cedar siding and a cultured stone foundation evoke cottage charm. Beyond the covered entry, a foyer holds the staircase to the 2,089-square-foot lower floor featuring two bedrooms and baths, a family room, and wetbar. To the left of the entry, the 2,203-square-foot main floor makes a grand statement in the dining and living rooms, which share a beamed, vaulted ceiling and a majestic stone fireplace. Transoms that follow the curve of the ceiling trusses admit plenty of light to both rooms. A pass-through buffet opens the dining room to the foyer. More arched passageways tie the dining and living rooms to the nearby kitchen and breakfast nook, making entertaining a breeze. The nook features bump-out windows that create an ideal spot for a built-in banquette. The master suite and a den are at one end of the home. A rotunda corridor directs traffic to the master bedroom, walk-in closet, and bath. This home is designed with a basement foundation.

ABOVE: Peaked gables and arches projecting from low, sloping roofs bring storybook cottage charm to the exterior of this home embellished with Craftsman details.

BELOW LEFT: The arch of the covered entry is repeated in windows and doorways throughout the home.

BELOW: In the kitchen, glass front cabinets top an arched pass through to the living room.

Order on-line at www.familyhomeplans.com

ABOVE: The two-sided flagstone fireplace is shared by the living and dining rooms.

ABOVE LEFT: A built-in buffet separates the formal dining room from the entry.

ABOVE RIGHT: The screen porch could easily be converted into a sunroom. A door opens from the porch onto a courtyard patio that's sheltered by the angled garage.

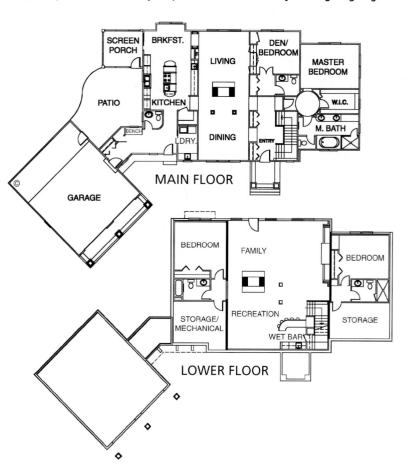

MAIN FLOOR

LOWER FLOOR

Plan Number 32298

Price Code	L
Total Finished	4,292 sq. ft.
Main Finished	2,203 sq. ft.
Lower Finished	2,089 sq. ft.
Garage Unfinished	780 sq. ft.
Porch Unfinished	132 sq. ft.
Dimensions	105'2"x71'
Foundation	Basement
Bedrooms	4
Full Baths	2
3/4 Baths	1
Half Baths	2

See thousands more plans at www.familyhomeplans.com

Craftsman 57

Arts & Crafts
Comfort

This home speaks of the classic Craftsman tradition throughout. Just inside the foyer is a beautifully made built-in bench flanked by see-through display cabinets with leaded-glass doors. While the dining room is rich in traditional Craftsman touches, such as the built-in china cabinets, box-beams, stenciling, and rich natural wood tones, straight across the hall, the two-story great room features the same sense of tradition, yet is somehow a bit more contemporary. On the 2,171-square-foot second floor, the master suite, with impressive bath and room-size walk-in closets, fills almost the entire front of the plan. A guest suite completes the area. To the rear, two secondary bedrooms share a full bath, each with access to their own vanity. Four porches and a sunroom add outdoor living space and a three-car garage includes additional storage space. This home is designed with a crawlspace foundation.

ABOVE: Low eaves, earthy colors, natural siding, and exposed rafter tails are trademark elements of Arts and Crafts design.

BELOW: Box beams, built-in china cabinets with leaded glass doors, stenciling, and lots of natural wood make a strong impression in the dining room.

ABOVE AND LEFT: The Craftsman tradition of natural wood finishes reaches a contemporary zenith in this large gourmet kitchen, exemplified by the hanging pot rack made of clear western fir. Square columns with wood trim transition the space to the two-story great room.

BELOW: Just inside the foyer, this built-in bench flanked by display cabinets—the result of first-class carpentry and careful attention to detail—separates the foyer from the formal dining room.

ABOVE: Although the woodwork in the great room is painted, unlike the more traditional natural woodwork in the rest of the home, the flavor of Arts and Crafts remains strongly anchored by the massive hand-laid stone fireplace and Craftsman mantle.

RIGHT AND BELOW: This private study at the front of the home brings out the best of Craftsman design with built-ins, earthy colors, and beautifully detailed woodwork.

Details clearly make a lot of difference in this home.

SECOND FLOOR

Craftsman details in the study mantel.

FIRST FLOOR

Inlaid wood and Craftsman detailing of the family room mantel.

Plan Number 91595

Price Code	L
Total Finished	4,283 sq. ft.
First Finished	1,642 sq. ft.
Second Finished	1,411 sq. ft.
Lower Finished	1,230 sq. ft.
Basement Unfinished	412 sq. ft.
Deck Unfinished	207 sq. ft.
Porch Unfinished	1,000 sq. ft.
Dimensions	92'x61'
Foundation	Basement
Bedrooms	4
Full Baths	3
3/4 Baths	1
Half Baths	1

A natural wood picture rail with hand-crafted support brackets in the study.

Leaded glass see-through doors flank the built-in bench in the foyer.

Painted box beams with stenciling in the dining room.

Inside Garden

The traditional exterior of this home belies the surprises that await within its strikingly modern floor plan. A full wall separates the formal dining room from the entry, but half walls open it up to the great room. A balcony in the wide-open great room overlooks the dramatic two-story atrium, which brightens up the main public rooms on both levels. The dining and utility areas fill the left wing of the 3,179-square-foot main floor, while a private section houses bedrooms on the right. Stairs descend through the atrium's garden space to the family room in the 2,546-square-foot walk-out lower floor. Additional bedrooms can be found on this level as well as a game area with bar. This home is designed with a basement foundation.

ABOVE & LEFT: Craftsman-inspired details such as low-pitched gabled roofs with wide overhanging eaves, square stone columns supporting the porch, and exposed ridge beams add traditional appeal to the exterior of this modern floor plan.

Plan Number 32342

Price Code	L
Total Finished	5,725 sq. ft.
Main Finished	3,179 sq. ft.
Lower Finished	2,546 sq. ft.
Basement Unfinished	633 sq. ft.
Garage Unfinished	881 sq. ft.
Dimensions	78'x72'
Foundation	Basement
Bedrooms	4
Full Baths	2
3/4 Baths	2
Half Baths	1

LOWER FLOOR

MAIN FLOOR

Southern

Porches and galleries played a significant part in shaping the architectural heritage of the south, where traditional Colonial styles were adapted to the climate by including large porch roofs to catch the breezes and shade the interior rooms. Galleries and raised basements were elements imported from the warm climate of the West Indies and adapted to vernacular farmhouses, French Colonial cottages, and medieval colonial styles similar to what we think of today as the Cape Cod.

The Southern style homes on the following pages reflect this rich tradition, maximizing living space both indoors and out, while opening up the interiors to include the spacious rooms and modern amenities today's homeowner expects from a finely crafted modern home.

Tropical MIx

Created for any climate but steeped in the regional architecture of Key West, Florida, this compact home makes the most of its 1,129 square feet and does it with style. Defining the home is a basic Cape Cod-style shape: a central gable structure with porches front and back. Outside, the home's wide trim, crown moldings, and deep sills create a vintage look. Inside, a sense of spaciousness is projected that reaches beyond the modest-sized home's actual dimensions. To maximize space, hallways are kept at a minimum and the living room, dining area, and kitchen all flow together around a central powder room. Out back is a long screen porch and wraparound deck. On the second floor, a smaller porch leads to a small deck off the rear. The secondary bedroom and master bedroom share the full bath. This home is designed with a crawlspace foundation.

ABOVE: The two-story porch lets light into the second floor but keeps out the sun during the hottest times of the year. Metal roofing and exposed rafter tails suggest the design's tropical roots.

BELOW: Counters and cabinetry surround the kitchen, offering plenty of work space.

RIGHT: Set into the longest wall in the open first-floor living and dining space, the fireplace becomes a central focal point. French doors on each side of the fireplace lead to a wraparound deck.

BELOW RIGHT: Privately nestled into the trees, the first-floor screen porch provides a shaded place to enjoy the backyard.

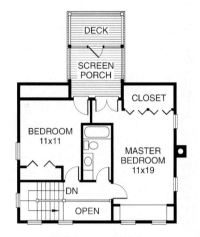

SECOND FLOOR

FIRST FLOOR

Plan Number 32399	
Price Code	A
Total Finished	1,129 sq. ft.
First Finished	576 sq. ft.
Second Finished	553 sq. ft.
Deck Unfinished	230 sq. ft.
Porch Unfinished	331 sq. ft.
Dimensions	36'8x36'
Foundation	Crawlspace
Bedrooms	2
Full Baths	1
Half Baths	1

ABOVE: A wide front porch with round columns and gabled dormers with working shutters embellish the facade of this classic cottage.

BELOW: The use of large arched doorways throughout the public spaces creates the sense of a traditional, well-crafted home, as illustrated by the elegant dining room.

Eastern Shore
Cottage

Careful planning and attention to detail are evident throughout this traditional cottage-style home, which offers every space a growing family might need. A deep, comfortable front porch leads into the home through a spacious foyer. Arched doorways open to the formal dining room at the front of the home and the vaulted great room at the rear. On the right side of the first floor, two secondary bedrooms share a hall bath. On the left side of the home, the master suite includes a sumptuous bath and two walk-in-closets. Utilitarian areas such as the kitchen pantry and laundry room are cleverly incorporated into the plan to be both convenient and unobtrusive. A large recreation room on the optional second floor shares space with a fourth bedroom, full bath, and plenty of attic storage. This home is designed with a basement foundation.

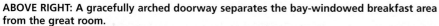

Plan Number 57001

Price Code	Please call for pricing
Total Finished	2,151 sq. ft.
First Finished	2,151 sq. ft.
Optional Second Unfinished	814 sq. ft.
Dimensions	61'x55'8"
Foundation	Basement
Bedrooms	3
Full Baths	2

ABOVE: Natural light floods the two-story great room from every level with dormers above and a wall of windows below. The built-in bookcase designed to look like a piece of furniture and the heavy mantel over the fireplace add rustic cottage charm to this soaring space.

ABOVE RIGHT: A gracefully arched doorway separates the bay-windowed breakfast area from the great room.

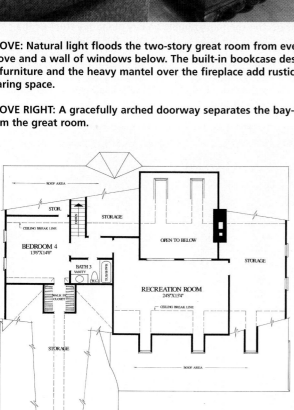

SECOND FLOOR

FIRST FLOOR

© William Poole Architects, Inc.

Double Galleries

Four covered porches provide this design with plenty of outdoor living space and create equally attractive facades for both the front and rear of the home. A center hall flanked by formal living and dining rooms leads straight back to a long family room at the rear. On the left side of the home, a butler's pantry connects the dining room to the kitchen, which is open to a window-lined breakfast room. A rear entrance just off the kitchen and breakfast area offers access to the laundry room and to the two car garage. On the second floor, the large master bedroom has a full width porch all to itself in addition to the usual amenities of a private bath and deep walk-in closet. Three additional bedrooms on this floor share two full baths between them. This home is designed with a crawlspace foundation.

ABOVE: The charming double gallery along the front of the house shades the interior rooms from the glare of the sun.

BELOW: The second floor gallery at the front of the home offers a cool, shady retreat for reading, relaxing, or rocking. A matching gallery at the rear of the home provides a secluded retreat for the master bedroom.

Plan Number 57036

Price Code	Please call for pricing
Total Finished	2,631 sq. ft.
First Finished	1,273 sq. ft.
Second Finished	1,358 sq. ft.
Dimensions	54'10"x48'6"
Foundation	Crawlspace
Bedrooms	4
Full Baths	3
Half Baths	1

ABOVE: The family room opens to a covered porch at the rear of the home.

RIGHT: Covered porches line the rear elevation as well as the front, providing ample shade and outdoor living space.

SECOND FLOOR

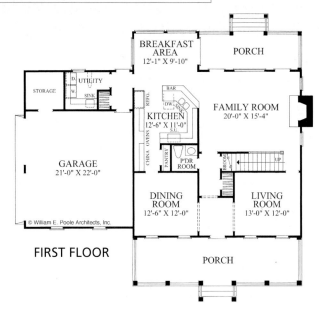

FIRST FLOOR

© William E. Poole Architects, Inc.

Photography & Line Art, courtesy of William E. Poole Architects, Inc.

Stylish Southern Cottage

ABOVE: A southern colonial cottage with gracious detailing in the porch, dormers, and entry door surround, provides a welcome sight in any neighborhood.

Charm, style, and comfort are the perfect words to describe this southern-style cottage. A lovely full-width front porch with elegant columns draws you in to a double-height center foyer flanked by formal living and dining rooms. Behind the dining room, an open counter-lined kitchen with large breakfast area and plenty of built-in storage opens to the fireplaced family room, which lies behind the living room. On the right side of the home, the secluded master suite sits across the hall from a convenient laundry room. The master bedroom, complete with his-and-her walk-in closets, is set apart from the main body of the house, maximizing privacy. Three secondary bedrooms, two full baths, and a future rec room over the two-car garage comprise the second floor. This home is designed with a crawlspace foundation.

Plan Number 57037

Price Code	Please call for pricing
Total Finished	2,806 sq. ft.
First Finished	1,927 sq. ft.
Second Finished	879 sq. ft.
Bonus Unfinished	459 sq. ft.
Dimensions	71'x53'
Foundation	Crawlspace
Bedrooms	4
Full Baths	3
Half Baths	1

FIRST FLOOR

SECOND FLOOR

Plan Number 32369

Price Code	D
Total Finished	2,930 sq. ft.
First Finished	1,770 sq. ft.
Second Finished	1,160 sq. ft.
Garage Unfinished	576 sq. ft.
Porch Unfinished	432 sq. ft.
Dimensions	66'x70'
Foundation	Crawlspace
Bedrooms	3
Full Baths	2
3/4 Baths	1

RIGHT AND BELOW: Tall windows and a wide front door with a classic surround of sidelights and elliptical fanlight opening up to a deep front porch provide a welcoming entry as well as a great place to enjoy a pleasant day. A trio of gabled dormers adds cottage appeal to the facade of this appealing brick home. White paint highlights the simple yet elegant trim details.

Classic and
Family Friendly

Inside its welcoming exterior, this home houses plenty of friendly space. The entry opens left into the formal dining room and straight ahead to the great room. The great room features a fireplace and large windows. The dining room offers convenient access to the utility areas in the far left wing of the home. In this wing, you'll find the laundry room, kitchen (defined by its ample counter space), and breakfast nook with French doors opening onto a rear screen porch. In the opposite wing rests the master suite—featuring a bay window, luxurious bath, and generous walk-in closet—and a secluded study, ideal for quiet work or relaxation. Two secondary bedrooms share the second floor with a playroom, full bath, and storage space. This home is designed with a crawlspace foundation.

FIRST FLOOR

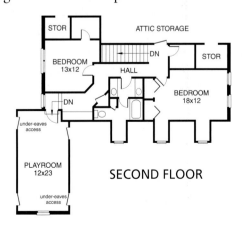

SECOND FLOOR

French Colonial Cottage

A wide covered porch offers a welcoming face to the neighborhood while shading the formal rooms at the front of the home. A center foyer opens up to the living room on the left through a wide doorway. Pocket doors close off the living room from a central hallway that connects the informal spaces at the rear of the home. To the right of the entry, the formal dining room, with elegant floor-to-ceiling windows, opens through a butler's pantry to the kitchen and the windowed breakfast area beyond. A big family room with a vaulted ceiling anchors the family spaces. The master suite is in its own wing and features an impressive walk-in-closet. On the second floor, three additional bedrooms, two full baths, and a future rec room space are joined together by a balcony that overlooks the family room. A utility room and a two-car garage with a storage room round out the first floor. This home is designed with a crawlspace foundation.

ABOVE: A steeply pitched hipped roof flares out at the eaves to cover the deep front porch in this handsome facade based on the French colonial cottages of the 1700s.

OPPOSITE: An abundance of windows and two sets of French doors open the family room up to the great outdoors.

BELOW: The floor-to-ceiling windows of the dining room are shaded by the covered porch at the front of the home.

ABOVE AND LEFT: The kitchen opens to the vaulted breakfast area where walls wrapped in windows make the space a sunroom.

Plan Number 57016

Price Code	Please call for pricing
Total Finished	3,102 sq. ft.
First Finished	2,142 sq. ft.
Second Finished	960 sq. ft.
Bonus Unfinished	327 sq. ft.
Dimensions	75'8"x53'
Foundation	Crawlspace
Bedrooms	4
Full Baths	3
Half Baths	1

ABOVE: The first floor master suite occupies its own wing.

BELOW: Windows fill the rear walls of the family room and breakfast area.

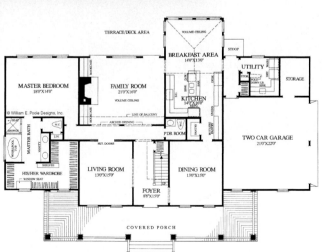

FIRST FLOOR

SECOND FLOOR

Comforts of Home

This Savannah cottage, or raised Colonial cottage, with its elegant columns and crowns, caps above windows, and classical front gable, is a beautiful example of traditional Southern architecture. This particular home was designed for a waterfront lot, where the house is open to the view, especially the living room, which opens onto the back porch through French doors. Transom windows over the door and windows to the porch help create a panoramic view. The master suite spreads out across the entire left wing of the 2,036-square-foot first floor. The master bath is ample and packed with amenities. The kitchen offers lots of light. Besides the light that flows in through the breakfast room, which has windows on three sides, double windows are installed over the sink. Off the corner of the kitchen is a walk-in pantry. On the 1,230-square-foot second floor, three bedrooms and two full baths fill three corners of the floor. A multimedia room occupies the fourth corner, with plenty of closet space throughout. This home is designed with a crawlspace foundation.

ABOVE: This classic Charleston-style home features five bedrooms, four baths, and spacious public rooms including a breakfast area, study, and large living room.

BELOW: This raised cottage offers lots of great outdoor space, including a large elevated deck and a big screen porch.

ABOVE: Glossy granite countertops add a touch of elegance to the kitchen. The door at the far right leads to a large corner pantry.

Plan Number 94699

Price Code	I
Total Finished	3,266 sq. ft.
First Finished	2,036 sq. ft.
Second Finished	1,230 sq. ft.
Deck Unfinished	88 sq. ft.
Porch Unfinished	756 sq. ft.
Dimensions	57'4"x59'
Foundation	Post
Bedrooms	5
Full Baths	3
Half Baths	1

ABOVE: This archway, supported by two slender Ionic columns, opens from the foyer into the dining room.

LEFT: From the living room, the symmetry of the view toward the front entryway is both classic and lovely. Light spills in from all sides thanks to the abundance of windows and glass-filled doors.

FIRST FLOOR

Wood Deck 29'3"x 10'
Screen Porch 28'5"x 8'
Master Bedroom 15'5"x 15'6"
Breakfast 11'4"x 17'6"
Living Room 22'x 16'6"
Kitchen
Study/Bedroom 12'8"x11'
Foyer
Dining 12'8"x 12'8"
Porch 47'x 12'

© Sater Design Collection

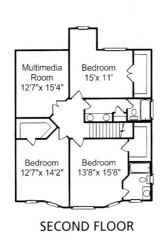

SECOND FLOOR

Multimedia Room 12'7"x 15'4"
Bedroom 15'x 11'
Bedroom 12'7"x 14'2"
Bedroom 13'8"x 15'8"

Photography: Chris A. Little

Southern Hospitality

ABOVE AND BELOW: The architectural elements of this traditional Southern raised cottage promise comfort and hospitality, from the tall roof down to the deep, shady, and welcoming front porch.

Designed and built in the style of the Southern raised cottage, this home manages to assemble all the necessary elements to create that time-honored sense of true Southern comfort.

The composition of tall and steep roof, narrow dormers, and a beautifully balustraded front porch creates a comforting sense of shelter —and a very strong sense of home.

A tall, arched front entry leads in to the foyer. Ahead, the living room is awash in light, thanks to two French doors that lead onto the back porch (and the arched transom lights above the French doors) as well as the full corner of light provided by the attached breakfast nook. The breakfast nook is open to the living room and kitchen— and to more windows. A balcony that opens part of the living room to the upstairs, provides even more illumination as well as depth of architectural detail.

To the left of the home is the kitchen/dining nook wing, which comes complete with cross breezes. Open the front door of the kitchen and let the breeze blow off the porch and all the way through to the back. At the rear of the kitchen wing is the breakfast nook, which is a sun-filled space for informal dining. For more formal occasions, the front dining room offers just the right atmosphere—you can entertain while the world goes by just outside the twin French doors that lead onto the front porch.

On the right side of the home is the master suite wing with its own porch. This wing runs deeper than the kitchen wing; it's also wider to make room for the spacious and comfortable master bedroom.

The master suite is beautifully proportioned, with a large, square bedroom, twin walk-in closets (hers is larger, of course) and a truly luxurious master bath with twin vanities and a discrete shower/water closet area. This home is designed with a basement foundation.

ABOVE: For formal dining, the main dining room of the home offers grandeur in the best Southern style. Twin French doors lead from the dining room onto the front porch.

LEFT: Beautiful built-ins, a classic mantle, hardwood flooring and a bank of French doors comprise a welcoming, comfortable living room.

BELOW: The foyer gives a quick glimpse into the level of detail this home possesses, from its abundant natural light to its classic architectural details.

ABOVE: The bead-board facing on the kitchen eating bar matches the wainscoting in the adjacent breakfast area.

RIGHT: A sunny corner of the kitchen wing is given over to the breakfast nook.

BELOW: Deep crown molding and beautiful wood cabinets and flooring establish a mood of comfort and hospitality in this deluxe gourmet kitchen.

Plan Number 94645

Price Code	H
Total Finished	3,335 sq. ft.
First Finished	2,129 sq. ft.
Second Finished	1,206 sq. ft.
Garage Unfinished	1,005 sq. ft.
Deck Unfinished	400 sq. ft.
Porch Unfinished	634 sq. ft.
Dimensions	59'4"x64'
Foundation	Basement
Bedrooms	4
Full Baths	4

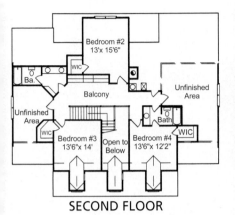

SECOND FLOOR

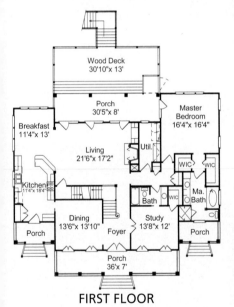

FIRST FLOOR

LOWER FLOOR

ABOVE: Spaciousness and light define the master bedroom, where you can wake up and step out onto the back porch through your private French doors to have coffee in the cool morning air.

BELOW: The rear of this raised Southern cottage-style home presents a completely different mood than the front. Here, there's the promise of privacy and shade, quiet time alone, and peaceful moments.

Private Garden

Outdoor rooms are plentiful in this spacious southern cottage, from the covered front porch, to the large rear deck, and the private garden off the master suite. And even the indoor rooms bring the outdoors in through the plentiful use of big windows. A wide foyer opens to the living room on the left and a library on the right. Behind the living room, a dining room with a large bay window offers an elegant spot for formal entertaining. Next to the dining room, an efficiently arranged kitchen opens to a long sunroom that features one of the home's three fireplaces. The right wing of the home houses a utility room and two-car garage. Behind this sits the luxurious master suite with its deep his-and-her walk-in closets, well-appointed bath, and access to a private, walled garden. There are three additional bedrooms on the second floor, one of which has a private full bath. The other two bedrooms share a bath. Also on the second floor is space for a future recreation room and a fifth bedroom with private bath. This home is designed with a crawlspace foundation.

ABOVE: This classic Southern cottage makes the most of indoor and outdoor spaces with a floor plan that includes a big covered porch, large deck, and a private garden off the master suite.

BELOW: The richly paneled library features a fireplace, built-in bookshelves, and a set of pocket doors that close it off from the family spaces at the rear of the home.

ABOVE: A big bay window brings light and views into the formal dining room.

BELOW: Arch-topped windows line the sunroom in the rear elevation.

SECOND FLOOR

Plan Number 57029

Price Code	Please call for pricing
Total Finished	3,901 sq. ft.
First Finished	2,648 sq. ft.
Second Finished	1,253 sq. ft.
Bonus Unfinished	355 sq. ft.
Dimensions	82'x60'4"
Foundation	Crawlspace
Bedrooms	4
Full Baths	3
Half Baths	1

FIRST FLOOR

Work and Play

Pillared porches, dormers, and classic archways embrace an open plan, creating a home in which the past flavors the present. An office sits to the right of the entry and another is located behind the garage. However, keeping with the theory that all work and no play is dull, the designer set the massive family room right in the middle, easily accessed from both studies. The left wing is a bit more formal, housing the living and dining rooms, as well as the master suite. In the center, the kitchen, defined by counter space, creates the hub of the home. Meanwhile on the second floor, two bedrooms share the space with a keeping room that has its own balcony and even more storage space. This home is designed with a slab foundation.

ABOVE: Attention to detail makes this Southern version of a Greek Revival home both unique and spectacular. Dormers adorned with round-top windows, old-fashioned molding, and columns supporting a deep front porch make it picture perfect.

BELOW: Step into your backyard and you'll feel as if you've traveled to a tropical island with your own veranda, balcony, and pool.

Order on-line at www.familyhomeplans.com

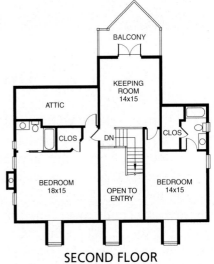

ABOVE: An arched niche in the dining room is the perfect spot for a sideboard or china cabinet.

LEFT: Arches repeated throughout the home in doorways and built-ins provide rich architectural texture.

SECOND FLOOR

FIRST FLOOR

Plan Number 32356

Price Code	L
Total Finished	4,042 sq. ft.
First Finished	2,822 sq. ft.
Second Finished	1,220 sq. ft.
Garage Unfinished	1,042 sq. ft.
Deck Unfinished	128 sq. ft.
Porch Unfinished	346 sq. ft.
Dimensions	96'8"x60'5"
Foundation	Slab
Bedrooms	3
Full Baths	3
Half Baths	1

Photography: Rick Taylor

Casual Elegance

With its wide-open spaces and easy traffic flow, this plan is ideal for entertaining. The front door with sidelights and an arched transom ushers guests inside where they have an immediate view of the formal dining room to the left and straight ahead to the family room. The family room's fireplace and built-ins are set to the side to allow a bank of windows to take over the rear wall.

In the kitchen, the cooktop island helps block the view of the food preparation area from the breakfast area. Past the breakfast area, French doors open onto a screen porch, extending the dining space in nice weather. Just off the screen porch, a corner deck offers additional outdoor living space. Other rooms on the 2,442-square-foot first floor include the master suite and a study.

Two bedrooms and two full baths are located on the 871-square-foot second floor. The bonus room adds 480 square feet. The lower floor (not shown) adds an additional 2,442 square feet. This home is designed with a basement foundation.

ABOVE: Mixed siding materials, clapboards and stone, create a rich texture. The long, shady porch is a welcoming spot to greet guests and neighbors.

BELOW: French doors extend the breakfast area onto the rear screen porch, for a comfortable spot in pleasant weather for any meal.

Order on-line at www.familyhomeplans.com

Plan Number 32358

Price Code	I
Total Finished	5,755 sq. ft.
First Finished	2,442 sq. ft.
Second Finished	871 sq. ft.
Lower Finished	2,442 sq. ft.
Bonus Unfinished	480 sq. ft.
Garage Unfinished	935 sq. ft.
Deck Unfinished	307 sq. ft.
Porch Unfinished	442 sq. ft.
Dimensions	72'6"x76'10"
Foundation	Basement
Bedrooms	3
Full Baths	3
Half Baths	1

ABOVE: A long kitchen island includes a cooktop and prep sink and helps distinguish the kitchen area from the adjacent open breakfast area. The windows over the sink look out over the rear deck.

BELOW: The entry and the upstairs hall remain light and open thanks to the entry's two-story height capped by a dormer. The doorway at left opens to the study.

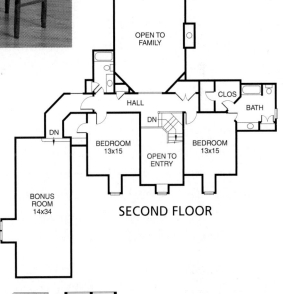

SECOND FLOOR

FIRST FLOOR

Farmhouse

Farmhouses across the country developed from a combined need for form and function with builders picking and choosing among the prevailing styles to develop a folk tradition that borrows predominately from Colonial, Greek Revival, and Victorian influences.

A number of the houses in our Colonial section could be considered New England farmhouses. Those houses follow more strictly the exterior formality of Colonial and Greek Revival architecture than the homes collected here. The houses for this section, while equally appealing, were specifically chosen for their more casual country charm.

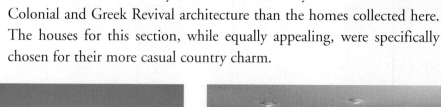

Optional Details

ABOVE: This charming vernacular farmhouse attracts attention thanks to its country classic wraparound porch, stacked front-facing gables, and dormer.

Perfect for a narrow lot, this home's rooms line up in the most livable manner. The entry opens to a foyer where columns mark entrances to the living and dining rooms. Down the hall, a work island separates the L-shape kitchen from the family room. The plan offers several options to make this the home of your dreams including a living room fireplace and a family room media unit. On the second floor, two secondary bedrooms are toward the front and the master suite fills the rear. Storage and closet space abound. This home is designed with basement, slab, and crawlspace foundation options.

Plan Number 99689

Price Code	B
Total Finished	1,635 sq. ft.
First Finished	880 sq. ft.
Second Finished	755 sq. ft.
Basement Unfinished	880 sq. ft.
Porch Unfinished	403 sq. ft.
Dimensions	36'x54'4"
Foundation	Basement Crawlspace Slab
Bedrooms	3
Full Baths	2
Half Baths	1

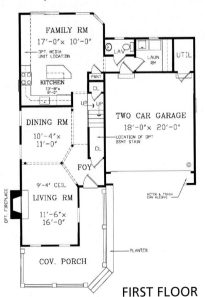

FIRST FLOOR

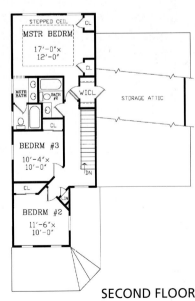

SECOND FLOOR

Thoughtfully
Designed

ABOVE: Classic architectural details and white trim accent the simple, traditional lines of this two-bedroom home.

BELOW: Tall windows, topped by transoms, form the walls in the breakfast nook, creating a light comfortable atmosphere ideal for casual meals.

A quartet of front-facing gables offers a welcoming, open facade to the street in this cozy farmhouse home. The front entry leads into a separate foyer that not only creates a formal entry but also provides a second interior door to prevent heat and air conditioning from escaping outdoors. This foyer, in turn, opens into a hallway offering equal access to the main floor as well as the staircase. Straight ahead to the rear of the home lies the kitchen, which opens into the casual dining area. A huge walk-in pantry and bath with laundry facilities is to the right. To the left of the design, a partial wall separates the kitchen from the family room, which also connects through a wide opening to the more formal dining area. Two bedrooms and lots of closet space share the second floor and a full bath. This home is designed with a basement foundation.

Order on-line at www.familyhomeplans.com

SECOND FLOOR

ABOVE LEFT: Tall windows, hardwood floors, and a secluded location lend a more formal atmosphere to the dining room.

ABOVE: The kitchen's long, two-tiered island separates the area from the breakfast nook, and provides ample work space and another casual place to dine.

BELOW: A triple set of windows brings light deep into the lovely living room.

FIRST FLOOR

Plan Number 65431

Price Code	C
Total Finished	1,980 sq. ft.
Dimensions	43'x53'4"
Foundation	Basement
Bedrooms	2
Full Baths	1
3/4 Baths	1

Elegantly Efficient

The inviting wraparound porch leads

to the main entry and an energy-efficient vestibule. To the left is a secluded study; to the right, the long living room with its lovely window. Beyond the living room is the formal dining area. This space leads into the kitchen, which is lined with counters and opens on the other end to a casual eating area. Steps away is the family room, which has a fireplace and two corners filled with windows.

On the second floor, a balcony overlooking the living room connects three bedrooms. A walk-in closet fills a corner of the master suite, which has a five-piece bath with a window illuminating the tub. The other two bedrooms have ample closet space, and share a full hall bath. This home is designed with a basement foundation.

ABOVE: Three covered porches with arches supported by square columns, front facing gables, and heavy window trim embellish the exterior of this classic country composition.

BELOW: Windows form the corners of the family room at the rear of the home, casting light over the hardwood floor and through the arched entry to the eating area of the kitchen.

Order on-line at www.familyhomeplans.com

ABOVE: An abundance of cabinets and a circular snack bar at the end of the counter make efficient use of space in the galley-style kitchen.

RIGHT: The large window in the living room heightens the feeling of spaciousness while the ample proportions of the room provides plenty of space for seating.

Plan Number 65138

Price Code	D
Total Finished	2,257 sq. ft.
First Finished	1,274 sq. ft.
Second Finished	983 sq. ft.
Garage Unfinished	437 sq. ft.
Deck Unfinished	339 sq. ft.
Porch Unfinished	183 sq. ft.
Dimensions	50'x46'
Foundation	Basement
Bedrooms	3
Full Baths	2
Half Baths	1

SECOND FLOOR

FIRST FLOOR

Pretty and **Practical**

Practicality mixes with beauty in this well-designed two-story home punctuated with built-ins. A tiled entry with closet ushers guests into the public spaces on the left side of the home. In the formal dining room, a built-in niche provides a place for a buffet or china cabinet. The great room, with its huge bay window and fireplace, is ideal for gatherings. Work space defines the efficient U-shape kitchen, which opens to the hearth room, where the fireplace casts its glow, and the window-lined breakfast room. The second floor is reserved for all four bedrooms. The master bedroom has its own compartmentalized bath and a deep walk-in closet. This home is designed with a basement foundation. Alternate foundation options available at an additional charge. Please call 1-800-235-5700 for more information.

ABOVE: A covered wraparound porch, front facing gables, and heavy trim give the exterior of this thoroughly modern home a touch of traditional country farmhouse appeal.

Plan Number 99457

Price Code	E
Total Finished	2,270 sq. ft.
First Finished	1,150 sq. ft.
Second Finished	1,120 sq. ft.
Basement Unfinished	1,150 sq. ft.
Garage Unfinished	457 sq. ft.
Dimensions	46'x48'
Foundation	Basement
Bedrooms	4
Full Baths	2
Half Baths	1

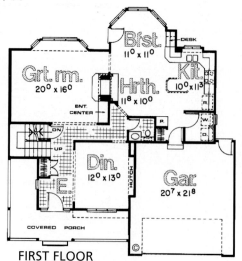

FIRST FLOOR

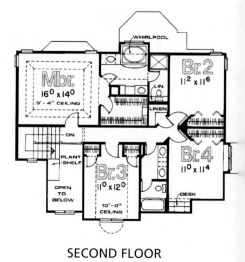

SECOND FLOOR

ABOVE: A center gable topping a quintet of windows is an ideal way to top off the classic wraparound porch.

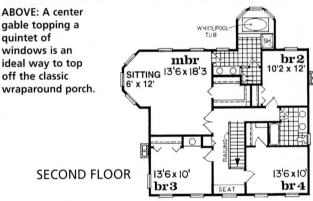

SECOND FLOOR

WHIRLPOOL TUB

SH

mbr 13'6 x 18'3

SITTING 6' x 12'

br 2 10'2 x 12'

RAILING

br 3 13'6 x 10'

SEAT

br 4 13'6 x 10'

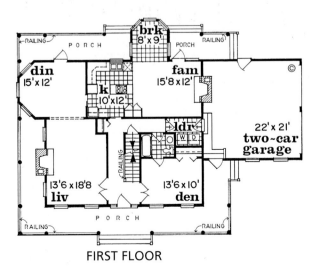

FIRST FLOOR

RAILING   PORCH   PORCH   RAILING

brk 8' x 9'

din 15' x 12'

k 10' x 12'

fam 15'8 x 12'

ldr   W D

22' x 21'
two~car garage

RAILING

liv 13'6 x 18'8

den 13'6 x 10'

RAILING   PORCH   RAILING

Farmhouse Flair

The wraparound porch not only provides space to enjoy the outdoors, it shelters the windows in the den and living room from direct sunlight while still keeping the spaces bright. A bay of windows defines the dining area, which opens to the kitchen. The kitchen blends into the breakfast area, also featuring a bay of windows, and the fireplace-warmed family room. All four bedrooms rest on the second floor where a window seat in the hall makes a nice quiet retreat. The master suite is a retreat in itself with a big bay of windows encompassing its sitting area and whirlpool tub. This home is designed with basement and crawlspace foundation options.

Plan Number 55005

Price Code	E
Total Finished	2,582 sq. ft.
First Finished	1,291 sq. ft.
Second Finished	1,291 sq. ft.
Basement Unfinished	1,291 sq. ft.
Garage Unfinished	495 sq. ft.
Porch Unfinished	709 sq. ft.
Dimensions	64'6"x47'
Foundation	Basement Crawlspace
Bedrooms	4
Full Baths	3

So Much Room

A classic floor plan offers three floors of indoor space while a deep wraparound porch and rear terrace allow comfortable outdoor living as well. Inside, each floor is designed for a specific purpose. The first floor is dedicated to the common living areas, yet keeps the formal living and dining rooms separate from the open family room, breakfast area, and kitchen space. The second floor houses the master suite and three additional bedrooms, each with ample closet space. The third floor is an "all-purpose room," which could serve as a game room, studio, additional bedroom, or whatever else you may require. This home is designed with basement and slab foundation options.

ABOVE: A deep wraparound porch lined with arch-topped windows extends living area outdoors. This version was modified to include an attractive gazebo adding to both the form and the function of this welcoming feature.

Plan Number 99649

Price Code	H
Total Finished	3,006 sq. ft.
First Finished	1,293 sq. ft.
Second Finished	1,138 sq. ft.
Third Finished	575 sq. ft.
Basement Unfinished	1,293 sq. ft.
Porch Unfinished	585 sq. ft.
Dimensions	63'4"x53'4"
Foundation	Basement
	Slab
Bedrooms	4
Full Baths	3
Half Baths	1

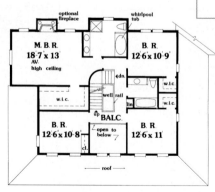

FIRST FLOOR

SECOND FLOOR

THIRD FLOOR

ABOVE: Wide cornice returns, varying roof lines, thoughtful window arrangements, a mix of stone and wood siding all combine to create a rich composition of texture and detail. A side-load garage enhances, rather than distracts from, the fine detailing and trim. Notice the "added-onto" feel of the small gable to the left, which houses the master bath.

BELOW: The addition of a screen porch wrapping around the breakfast room and keeping room adds to living space while maintaining the architectural integrity of this attractive rear elevation.

Country
Perfect

The spacious foyer with a winding staircase opens into a spacious family room and, to the right, the formal dining room. To the rear of the home is the kitchen with attached breakfast room that's set into a deep bay. In a line with the family room and kitchen area is the keeping room which, like the family room, contains a fireplace. Rounding out the floor is the master suite, which features twin walk-in closets and a well-appointed bath. On the generous second floor, three secondary bedrooms share space with a reading loft, bonus area, and two bathrooms. Plenty of windows fill the home with warmth and light. This home is designed with a basement foundation.

ABOVE: The formal dining room, set apart at the front of the home, features a deep bay window and elegant trim. A butler's pantry connects the room to the kitchen.

RIGHT: An open staircase leads from the wide entry to the second floor. Tall windows light the landing.

BELOW: A great kitchen layout makes efficient use of a space roughly the same size as the dining room. Cabinets built into the counters that separate the kitchen from the breakfast area provide attractive functionality.

Plan Number 32437

Price Code	I
Total Finished	3,330 sq. ft.
First Finished	2,021 sq. ft.
Second Finished	1,309 sq. ft.
Basement Unfinished	2,021 sq. ft.
Garage Unfinished	484 sq. ft.
Dimensions	64'6"x46'6"
Foundation	Basement
Bedrooms	4
Full Baths	2
3/4 Baths	1
Half Baths	1

ABOVE: An impressive arrangement of windows and French doors provides a wall of light and outdoor views for the family room that can be seen from the front door.

ABOVE RIGHT: A heavy soffit with deep crown molding and vaulted ceiling showcase an arched window above French doors in the secluded master bedroom.

RIGHT: The master bath features a garden tub set into a deep bay beneath a vaulted ceiling. Two walk-in-closets complete the first floor master suite.

FIRST FLOOR

SECOND FLOOR

Memorable Country

The long, wraparound porch sets just the tone for this excellent example of traditional country farmhouse design, which comes filled with generously-sized shared spaces and plenty of privacy to boot.

The home's entry is flanked by the living room to the left and the formal dining room to the right; straight ahead, stairs lead to the 1,555-square-foot second floor. Guests can be led either down the hall that opens into the dining room and straight into the breakfast and kitchen areas, or through the living room into the family room.

A spacious, U-shape kitchen includes an island and a small planning desk. The adjacent breakfast area offers table room inside a bay window. Past the kitchen and laundry, a discrete home office could become a guest room. For convenience, the three-car garage opens into the hallway outside the laundry room. The entire first floor comprises 1,868 square feet of living area.

Upstairs are the three secondary bedrooms. Carved out of the second floor is the master suite, which takes up one corner of the second floor and extends into the wide space over the three-car garage. This home is designed with a basement foundation.

See thousands more plans at www.familyhomeplans.com

Plan Number 32036

Price Code	I
Total Finished	3,423 sq. ft.
First Finished	1,868 sq. ft.
Second Finished	1,555 sq. ft.
Garage Unfinished	740 sq. ft.
Dimensions	67'x48'6"
Foundation	Basement
Bedrooms	4
Full Baths	2
3/4 Baths	1
Half Baths	1

SECOND FLOOR

FIRST FLOOR

ABOVE: Shaded by the wraparound porch, the formal dining room remains cool but still captures plenty of natural light from the adjacent two-story foyer.

BELOW: The big stone fireplace adds just the right touch of country to this comfortable family room.

Photography: Jim Hedrich, Hedrich-Blessing

Photography: James Yochum Photography

spacious Cottage

ABOVE: A trellis covered deck, sunporch, and second floor screen porch are tucked between twin gables at the rear of the home.

BELOW: The light filled dining room is at the center of this casual, open floor plan.

Steep gables, quaint dormers, French doors, and elegant columns combine classic elements of old-house charm with today's best architectural innovations. The angled entry is nestled into the crook of the home's L-shape footprint. Inside the entry, angles in the living room and a wide arc of windows and French doors in the sunporch provide a light-filled, comforting setting. At the front of the home, a private library features built-ins bookshelves. The dining room shares a double-sided fireplace with the living room. In the kitchen, a triangular island mimics the shape of a nearby walk-in pantry. On the second floor, the master suite features two roomy walk-in closets and access to a screen porch. Three additional bedrooms complete the second floor. This home is designed with a basement foundation.

Plan Number 32337

Price Code	E
Total Finished	3,756 sq. ft.
First Finished	2,038 sq. ft.
Second Finished	1,718 sq. ft.
Basement Unfinished	1,629 sq. ft.
Porch Unfinished	144 sq. ft.
Dimensions	52'x59'4"
Foundation	Basement
Bedrooms	4
Full Baths	2
Half Baths	2

LEFT: The rounded wall of the sunporch is lined with windows and French doors.

BELOW LEFT: Arched doorways flank the double-sided fireplace in the home's living room, which takes up one wing of the first floor.

BELOW: Climbing vines around an arched pergola, potted roses, and mature trees are fitting accents for the Victorian-style exterior of this home.

SECOND FLOOR

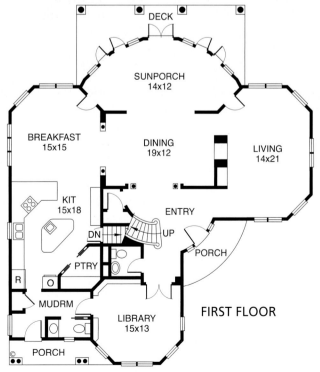

FIRST FLOOR

Photography: David W. Brown

Wide Dormers

Lovely, wide shed dormers dominate the visual features on this Cape-style home's exterior. The dormer across the front draws light into the upstairs as well as into the first floor, thanks to its position overlooking a loft and the home's open stairwell. The rear dormer brings light into the second floor. The garage also gets light from the sun, provided by a third shed dormer. Meanwhile, a wide porch across the front of the home offers a warm welcome to visitors.

Inside this 4,205-square-foot home, spaces and functions are clearly defined. The center of the first floor is all public, shared space, from the large entry hall to the dining room to the great room. The sunken great room overlooks the large deck and backyard through a wide wall of windows. Up two steps to the front are the dining room and entry, which are visually separated by wainscoted columns; two steps to the left is the breakfast room. A big stone hearth is the dramatic focal point of the great room; it shares its wall with two built-in storage units. The left side of the plan comprises more functional purposes. The garage, laundry, powder room, office area, kitchen, and breakfast room all line up along an angled axis. Taking up the right side of the 2,707-square-foot first floor is the master suite, which includes a 300-square-foot master bedroom and large bath with spacious walk-in closet, as well as a discrete study and a second full bath. This home is designed with a crawlspace foundation.

ABOVE: Sheltering dormers and a broad front porch create a welcoming entryway to this home. To the left, a separate dormer brings light into the two-car garage, which includes a bump-out large enough to hold a workbench.

BELOW: The long kitchen offers plenty of counter space and an angled eating bar that's open to the breakfast room. A hallway lined with utility spaces such as an office and a laundry room connects the kitchen to the two-car garage.

See thousands more plans at www.familyhomeplans.com

RIGHT AND BELOW RIGHT: A broad expanse of windows and French doors draw light into the sunken great room. Steps lead down from the central hall and the window-lined breakfast area into the open space, which includes a stone fireplace with built-in storage.

Plan Number 32345

Price Code	L
Total Finished	4,205 sq. ft.
First Finished	2,707 sq. ft.
Second Finished	1,498 sq. ft.
Garage Unfinished	651 sq. ft.
Deck Unfinished	848 sq. ft.
Porch Unfinished	465 sq. ft.
Dimensions	74'8"x96'
Foundation	Crawlspace
Bedrooms	4
Full Baths	4
3/4 Baths	2

SECOND FLOOR

FIRST FLOOR

RIGHT: Overlooking the deck and beyond, an abundance of windows defines the rear of the home.

Photography: Courtesy of the Designer

Great American
Tradition

ABOVE: This traditional design offers a comfortable country lifestyle and lots of outdoor space.

BELOW: The kitchen opens to a big, window-lined breakfast area with access to a covered rear porch.

Melding a pleasing variety of traditional American styles, this mix of Georgian and colonial results in both a satisfying and a highly functional home that builds nicely on its historical country roots.

Mixed with ample private areas are large shared spaces, among them a big family room with hearth and coffered ceiling, a living room that opens to the two-story foyer and dining room beyond, and an efficient kitchen plan that includes a sunny breakfast room. Upstairs is a 340-square-foot playroom for the kids.

The 2,372-square-foot second floor is dominated by the master suite with tray ceiling, a huge master bath with vaulted ceiling, a secluded porch, and private sitting room that overlooks the backyard. Three secondary bedrooms, one with a private bath and the others with a cleverly designed shared bath, round out the second floor.

This home is designed with basement and crawlspace foundation options.

See thousands more plans at www.familyhomeplans.com

ABOVE: At nearly 265 square feet, the master bath has room for all the modern amenities including an oversized shower and separate oversized tub, a skylight and complete twin vanities.

LEFT: With its recessed sideboard niche, wainscoting, arched entry, and deep crown molding, the formal dining room is an interesting counterpoint to the home's informal areas.

BELOW: A full retreat is available in the master bedroom suite, which includes a spacious bedroom with adjoining sitting room and three-sided peninsula fireplace.

Plan Number 60137

Price Code	L
Total Finished	4,464 sq. ft.
First Finished	2,092 sq. ft.
Second Finished	2,372 sq. ft.
Basement Unfinished	2,092 sq. ft.
Garage Unfinished	674 sq. ft.
Dimensions	75'5"x64'
Foundation	Basement
	Crawlspace
Bedrooms	5
Full Baths	4
Half Baths	1

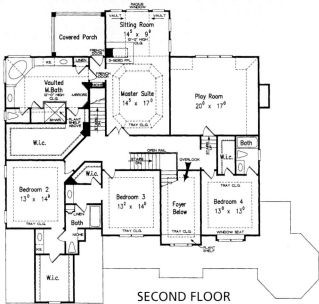

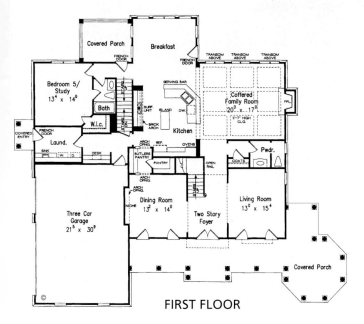

FIRST FLOOR

SECOND FLOOR

Photography: Craig Dugan, Hedrich-Blessing

Wall of Windows

A beautiful layout and careful planning create a home that's ideal for entertaining. The formal living and dining rooms sit just inside the entry, with a powder room just steps away. Further back, a long hallway connects the library to the kitchen/breakfast area, passing the spacious family room along the way. The outside wall of the family room is made up of tall windows and includes a large hearth. A second fireplace warms the living room. Bedrooms make up the entire 1,820-square-foot second floor. Each has a walk-in closet and both the master suite and a secondary bedroom have private baths. The master suite also features a bay window in the bedroom and a five-piece private bath. Plenty of room for vehicles and storage is provided by the 702-square-foot side-load garage. This home is designed with a basement foundation.

ABOVE: Varied window sizes and shapes accent the front facade, which is clad in a mix of shingle and stone siding.

BELOW: Multiple gables and banks of windows form a pleasing composition in this handsome rear elevation.

See thousands more plans at www.familyhomeplans.com

ABOVE: Windows flanking the living room fireplace and a big box window at the front of the room fill the space with light.

LEFT: The use of heavy moldings adds textural appeal to the formal dining room.

BELOW: Country casual reigns in the vaulted family room where a tall, curving bay of windows enhances both the interior of the space and the exterior of the house.

ABOVE: Rich wood bookcases, trim moldings, and plantation shutters add depth and warmth to the library

ABOVE RIGHT: The luxurious master bath maintains a cottage feel from transom windows and varying ceiling angles that follow the roof line of the gable into which it is nestled.

RIGHT: Angled walls of windows frame the spacious master bedroom.

BELOW: The built-in linen closet at the head of the stairs.

Order on-line at www.familyhomeplans.com

ABOVE AND RIGHT: A combination kitchen and breakfast area at the rear of the home is open to the family room creating one continuous space ideal for casual entertaining as well as family togetherness. Light wood cabinetry looks rich but keeps the space bright and light.

Plan Number 32426

Price Code	L
Total Finished	5,124 sq. ft.
First Finished	1,902 sq. ft.
Second Finished	1,820 sq. ft.
Lower Finished	1,402 sq. ft.
Basement Unfinished	424 sq. ft.
Garage Unfinished	702 sq. ft.
Dimensions	71'4"x58'4"
Foundation	Basement
Bedrooms	4
Full Baths	3
Half Baths	1

FIRST FLOOR

FAMILY 17x19
KITCHEN/BRKFST 25x16
GARAGE 12x20
LIBRARY 12x14
DN
UP
LAUNDRY
LIVING 13x16
ENTRY
DINING 13x17
GARAGE 20x22

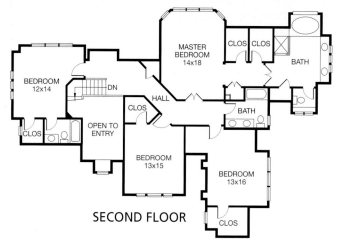

SECOND FLOOR

BEDROOM 12x14
CLOS
MASTER BEDROOM 14x18
CLOS CLOS
BATH
DN
HALL
CLOS
OPEN TO ENTRY
BATH
BEDROOM 13x15
BEDROOM 13x16
CLOS

Casual
Sophistication

The unpretentious exterior only hints at this home's sophisticated, yet family-friendly floor plan. The heart of this home is a central open area on the 3,772-square-foot first floor, where the great-room and kitchen function as one space. An L-shape island sections off the kitchen work space. A sunny dining room, with space for a hutch, is within view of the kitchen. French doors in the massive great room open onto the rear porch. A full bath, accessible from the backyard sits nearby. The master suite is isolated behind the garage beyond a window-lined hallway. The study has double doors that close it off from the rest of the common areas. On the 1,842-square-foot second floor, three secondary bedrooms share space with two baths and 950 square feet of bonus space. This home is designed with basement and crawlspace foundation options.

Photography: Michael Partenio

See thousands more plans at www.familyhomeplans.com

ABOVE: The private study, which could also serve as a formal living room or parlor, features a bay window and fireplace.

LEFT: A simple yet elegantly detailed staircase graces the large entry hall.

BELOW: Comfy furnishings fill the vaulted great room. The owners added a fireplace and built-ins on an exterior wall.

ABOVE: Even the range hood looks like well-crafted furniture in this country perfect kitchen.

ABOVE RIGHT: The dining room is decorated in a relaxed style to complement the country casual feel of the home. A built-in niche is the perfect place to house a china cabinet or hutch.

BELOW RIGHT: Marble counter tops, wood cabinets with crown moldings, under-counter cabinets with bead board siding, and sleek stainless appliances create an engaging textural continuity in the big kitchen at the hub of the home.

BELOW: Slide out shelves make a great alternative to drawers in these attractive under counter cabinets.

ABOVE: The owners enclosed the porch located behind the great room. The porch opens to a rear patio and pool, creating a resort right in the backyard.

LEFT: A bay window makes a sunny sitting area in the long master bedroom, secluded in its own wing at the rear of the home.

Plan Number 32373

Price Code	L
Total Finished	5,614 sq. ft.
First Finished	3,772 sq. ft.
Second Finished	1,842 sq. ft.
Bonus Unfinished	950 sq. ft.
Basement Unfinished	2,595 sq. ft.
Garage Unfinished	1,022 sq. ft.
Porch Unfinished	481 sq. ft.
Dimensions	120'8"x95'3"
Foundation	Basement Crawlspace
Bedrooms	4
Full Baths	3
3/4 Baths	1
Half Baths	1

*This home cannot be built in the state New York.

FIRST FLOOR

SECOND FLOOR

Photography: Emily J. Followill

Beautifully
Deceptive

From the outside, this stone-and-cedar-shingle home looks like a snug cottage. But inside it is deceptively spacious. Easy flowing spaces on the 3,020-square-foot first floor include a large kitchen that overlooks the front yard, a living room with a fireplace, and a media room and dining room joined together at the back of the home. For working at home, an office, conference area, and bath are set into the space above the garage on the first floor; this space has easy access to the kitchen and a separate entrance. The master suite and a secondary bedroom are on the opposite end of the home. Dormers create quaint niches in the bedrooms and game room on the 1,892-square-foot second floor. Each second floor bedroom includes a walk-in closet and private bath access. The game room is spacious enough to house areas for homework and play. The 1,314-square-foot lower floor provides space for casual entertaining in its recreation room, plus a wetbar and wine cellar. The garage connects to a workroom, which opens to a storage area. This home is designed with basement and crawlspace foundation options.

ABOVE: A combination of cedar shingle and stone siding, gable and shed dormers, window molding, and shutters dress up the exterior.

BELOW: The rustic fieldstone fireplace is capped by a hand-hewn oak mantel, which contrasts nicely with the sophisticated charm of the living room.

See thousands more plans at www.familyhomeplans.com

ABOVE: A built in window seat offers storage and a cozy retreat in the kitchen.

RIGHT: A triple-set of arch-topped windows sheds light over the eating area and the whole kitchen.

BELOW: The kitchen is full of storage space and useful touches such as the island, which provides extra room for preparation and casual dining.

ABOVE: The big master bedroom is separated from the main body of the house and offers direct access to the rear covered porch.

RIGHT: Plenty of counter space and storage offers clutter-free convenience in the master bath.

BELOW: A first floor bedroom in the same wing as the master suite serves as a convenient nursery.

Plan Number 32401

Price Code	L
Total Finished	6,226 sq. ft.
First Finished	3,020 sq. ft.
Second Finished	1,892 sq. ft.
Lower Finished	1,314 sq. ft.
Garage Unfinished	810 sq. ft.
Porch Unfinished	461 sq. ft.
Dimensions	79'6"x60'6"
Foundation	Basement
	Crawlspace
Bedrooms	6
Full Baths	5
3/4 Baths	1

ABOVE: The covered porch at the rear of the home opens off the master bedroom and the media room and could easily be converted to a screen porch.

LEFT: Three bedrooms on the second floor open out to a large game room, here used as a playroom for the children of the family.

Modification Tip: The plans include a side wing with lower level garage and main level bonus suite. Tucking the garage under the main level and eliminating this wing would allow the home to fit smaller lots and smaller budgets. The basement could be designed to accommodate up to three cars and still have space for a rec room, storage, and mechanicals.

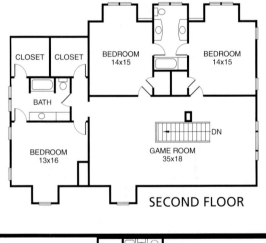

Traditional

Front facing gables, wide molding and cornice returns, keystones, fanlights, Palladian windows—the gamut of ornamentation is brought to today's housing creating a new and unique American vernacular steeped in a rich architectural heritage. The classic elements used to adorn the exteriors of these homes lend an air of permanence and tradition to the developing suburban landscape while combining those elements in fresh and original ways.

Open floor plans, volume ceilings, and two-story spaces are all hallmarks of the new tradition. Spacious master suites and abundant closet space can be found in every plan in this book, no matter how authentically period the exterior may appear, yet it was the eclectic American traditional style that introduced these elements and created the demand. Some of the finest examples available today from the nation's best architects and designers are featured on the following pages.

Spacious
Elegance

This spacious home reflects a high standard of living and a wealth of inspired architectural detail. The large two-story foyer leads directly into the dining room on the right and the formal living room on the left, both of which feature decorative ceilings. Straight ahead lies the two-story grand-room, visually distinguished by a pair of elegant columns. The open kitchen is filled with all the modern amenities, including a central island that provides additional work space. The master suite takes up a good part of the left side of the first floor and features a luxurious private bath topped by many built-in plant shelves. This home is designed with basement and slab foundation options.

Plan Number 93606	
Price Code	H
Total Finished	3,029 sq. ft.
First Finished	2,115 sq. ft.
Second Finished	914 sq. ft.
Basement Unfinished	2,115 sq. ft.
Garage Unfinished	448 sq. ft.
Dimensions	60'x52'
Foundation	Basement Slab
Bedrooms	4
Full Baths	3
Half Baths	1

SECOND FLOOR

ABOVE: This home's facade, featuring a quartet of gables, arched-topped windows, keystones, and brick hints of the detail found inside.

FIRST FLOOR

Stately Exterior—
Modern Interior

This-two story brick home features the old fashioned look of turn-of-the-century homes mixed with a contemporary floor plan. The bright two story foyer with angled staircase is framed by an elegant dining room to the left and a study on the right. A generous kitchen lined with counters opens into a breakfast bay perfect for reading the morning paper. The master suite features a polygonal sitting area that makes a perfect get-away. Upstairs you'll enjoy a dramatic view of both the foyer and the family room below as you cross the bridge to any of the three additional bedrooms, all with walk-in closets and one with a private bath. This home is designed with a basement foundation.

ABOVE: A barrel-vault covered entry between twin brick gables offers an elegant face to the street. Neoclassical details in the elliptical fanlight with sidelights surrounding the front door and the wide cornice moldings contribute to the attractiveness of the home.

Plan Number 93118

Price Code	I
Total Finished	3,397 sq. ft.
First Finished	2,385 sq. ft.
Second Finished	1,012 sq. ft.
Basement Unfinished	2,385 sq. ft.
Garage Unfinished	846 sq. ft.
Dimensions	79'x55'
Foundation	Basement
Bedrooms	4
Full Baths	3
Half Baths	1

*This plan is not to be built within a 75-mile radius of Cedar Rapids, IA.

FIRST FLOOR

SUNROOM 11'-0" x 13'-0"
EATING AREA 11'-0" x 8'-0"
KITCHEN 19'-0" x 14'-0"
FAMILY ROOM 20'-0" x 18'-0"
MASTER BEDROOM 19'-0" x 14'-0"
SITTING AREA 10'-0" x 8'-0"
4 CAR GARAGE 21'-0" x 38'-0"
DINING ROOM 15'-0" x 13'-0"
STUDY 12'-0" x 12'-0"
FOYER

SECOND FLOOR

OPEN TO FAMILY RM.
BEDROOM #2 17'-0" x 12'-0"
BEDROOM #4 13'-0" x 13'-0"
OPEN TO FOYER
BEDROOM #3 17'-0" x 12'-0"

Spacious and
Gracious

ABOVE: Stacked gables and a mix of brick, stone, and lap siding add interesting texture to the facade of this spacious home.

BELOW: The library at the front of the home is off to the side of the main areas of daily living, offering a quiet space for more solitary pursuits. The room opens to both the foyer and the master suite.

A library beside the open, welcoming foyer also opens through double doors into the spacious master suite, offering privacy and seclusion whenever it's needed. A coffered, barrel-vaulted ceiling crowns the impressive two-story great room, which features a fireplace surrounded by paneled built-ins. Another fireplace warms a combination breakfast/hearth room, which is open to a large, well-planned kitchen. Adjoining the kitchen is a large pantry opposite the laundry room. A second-floor computer loft with a built-in desk links three more bedrooms. This home is designed with a basement foundation.

ABOVE: Rich architectural detailing highlights this impressive double-height barrel-vaulted great room. This view looking toward the foyer shows the impressive fireplace surrounded by wonderful built-ins.

RIGHT: The view of the great room from the hall highlights the beautiful ceiling, elegant windows and the second floor computer loft.

BELOW: The breakfast/hearth room just off the kitchen provides a casual space for the family.

ABOVE: Kitchen cabinetry maintains the custom look of built-in furniture due to varying heights and the use of architectural trim and moldings. A center island beautifully adds to the work and storage space. Notice the ample task lighting provided throughout the kitchen under the cabinets and recessed in the ceiling ensuring that no work space is left in the dark. Windows line the adjacent breakfast/hearth room flooding the entire space with natural light.

SECOND FLOOR

FIRST FLOOR

Plan Number 97791

Price Code	J
Total Finished	3,746 sq. ft.
First Finished	2,665 sq. ft.
Second Finished	1,081 sq. ft.
Basement Unfinished	2,665 sq. ft.
Garage Unfinished	766 sq. ft.
Deck Unfinished	289 sq. ft.
Porch Unfinished	320 sq. ft.
Dimensions	88'x52'6"
Foundation	Basement
Bedrooms	4
Full Baths	2
3/4 Baths	1
Half Baths	1

Solid **Beauty**

Ample spaces and creature comforts are wrapped inside the rock-solid traditional exterior of this home, which speaks of success and contentment.

The centerpiece of the home is the living area, a 20x14-foot anchoring place for family and friends that's filled with natural light and seems to extend itself onto the large rear wraparound deck due to a bank of four windows and doorway. The living area is wide open to the two-story entry and formal dining room, which all work together to create a single large space for family or social get-togethers. The highlight of the kitchen area is the breakfast nook, a 14x11-foot sunroom that's virtually built of windows.

Also on this side of the home is the generously sized laundry room and the three-car garage, which includes its own enclosed storage area and full bath, just the place for cleaning up after sports or yard work.

The master bedroom, which is large enough for both bed and a cozy sitting area, includes a private fireplace. Two walk-in closets flank the plush master bath that includes a big soaking tub and twin vanities. Fronting the master suite is the private study.

Upstairs are three good-sized bedrooms, two full baths, plenty of closet space, a private study, and a large playroom. The home is designed with a crawlspace foundation.

ABOVE: The updated traditional exterior of this fine brick home signals both comfort and material accomplishment. The garage opens to the side of home to prevent the three garage doors from dominating the front facade.

BELOW: The master bedroom is large enough to include a cozy sitting area in front of the fireplace. Built-in cabinets above the mantel hide the television.

Plan Number 32295

Price Code	K
Total Finished	3,754 sq. ft.
First Finished	2,234 sq. ft.
Second Finished	1,520 sq. ft.
Garage Unfinished	918 sq. ft.
Deck Unfinished	462 sq. ft.
Porch Unfinished	144 sq. ft.
Dimensions	83'8"x63'
Foundation	Crawlspace
Bedrooms	4
Full Baths	3
3/4 Baths	1
Half Baths	1

ABOVE: Plenty of built-ins provide all the necessary storage space in this highly-functional kitchen, which wraps around the two-tiered kitchen island.

ABOVE RIGHT: Like the home's own private solarium, the sun-filled breakfast room is wrapped in tall windows and includes two doors onto the deck that wraps around the space.

RIGHT: A wall of windows, plus access to the rear deck, fill the large living area with natural light. A traditional fireplace flanked by floor-to-ceiling built-ins is the centerpiece of the room.

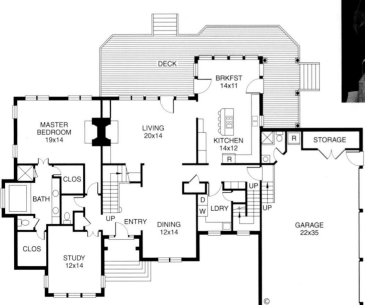

FIRST FLOOR

SECOND FLOOR

Great **Rooms**

ABOVE: A quintet of gables punctuating the front elevation paint a charming and welcoming portrait of a comfortable standard-of-living.

Spacious and comfortable, open and light, with well-separated private and shared spaces, this home rings of entertaining, big family gatherings, and life lived on a large scale. The 2,727-square-foot first floor includes the great room, family room, dining room and grand entry as well as first-floor living for the grown-ups of the family. Throw in a powder room, laundry, guest suite with full bath, large rear deck, covered patio, two-car garage, and wide front porch, and the plan for the first floor alone fills the functional requirements for most lifestyles.

The layout of the master suite is a masterpiece of organization. Comprising roughly one-fourth of the first floor, the suite carefully separates functions to provide maximum comfort and efficiency. The suite is well insulated from the main public areas of the home—the wall that separates the master bedroom from the great room comprises a fireplace flanked by a full wall of built-ins to ensure low sound penetration. The suite's walk-in closets are at diagonal opposites inside the ample master bath, which also separates the bath's twin vanities as far as possible, thereby increasing efficiency and improving the flow as two adults prepare for their day simultaneously. A separate shower enclosure and an enclosed water closet round out the useful features of the bath. There's also a small private porch, which is accessible only from the master bedroom.

Upstairs, via one of the home's two staircases, are 1,168 square feet of additional living space. Two secondary bedrooms share a full bath while a third is a suite, with walk-in closet and a full, private bath, making it ideal for an in-law suite or room for an older child. A large walk-in closet in one of the secondary bedrooms opens onto a 100-square-foot bonus area, which could become a study room, entertainment room or secret hideaway for some lucky child. Tucked away on the other side of the secondary bedrooms is a finished office space. This home is designed with a basement foundation.

ABOVE: Great lines define the quality of this home, starting with the stairway just inside the entryway.

RIGHT: Under a raised ceiling, an enormous arched window, transom-topped French doors, and a classic fireplace surround give the living room an air of elegant formality.

BELOW: Light filters into the entry from above, adding light and warmth. The arch of the door surround is repeated in the big living room window.

ABOVE: Light-filled and efficient, the kitchen includes a sit-down island for informal meals.

LEFT: The window-lined breakfast area with window seat is an ideal place to dine or relax.

OPPOSITE: Exposed trusswork, tall windows crowned with transom lights, a brick fireplace, and a French door onto the rear deck form a comfortable setting in the spacious great room.

Plan Number 32146

Price Code	K
Total Finished	3,895 sq. ft.
First Finished	2,727 sq. ft.
Second Finished	1,168 sq. ft.
Bonus Unfinished	213 sq. ft.
Basement Unfinished	2,250 sq. ft.
Garage Unfinished	984 sq. ft.
Deck Unfinished	230 sq. ft.
Porch Unfinished	402 sq. ft.
Dimensions	73'8"x72'2"
Foundation	Basement
Bedrooms	5
Full Baths	4
Half Baths	1

PATIO

FAMILY
15x19

DECK

PORCH

BRKFST
12x10

MASTER
BEDROOM
15x18

CLOS

UP

GREAT-
ROOM
18x16

KIT
18x14

BATH

DN

CLOS

O R

W D P

LDRY

DINING
12x17

ENTRY

GUEST/
STUDY
14x11

UP

GARAGE
20x14

PORCH

FIRST FLOOR

OPEN TO
FAMILY

OFFICE
10x13

OPEN TO
GREAT-
ROOM

BEDROOM
12x12

DN

BRIDGE

DN

BEDROOM
12x18

CLOS

BEDROOM
12x14

OPEN TO
ENTRY

BONUS
ROOM
10x19

SECOND FLOOR

Traditional

Rhapsody in **Brick**

This perfect family home offers plenty of well-planned spaces for daily living. The formal dining and living rooms flank the entry, both enjoying natural light through wide windows. A fireplace warms the large family room, which also has a door to the spacious rear deck. The kitchen's wraparound serving bar can be admired from a built-in banquette in the breakfast room's bay window. Beyond the breakfast room, a keeping room, with one of the home's three fireplaces, also accesses the rear deck. A three-car garage rounds out the first floor. A second-floor hall connects three bedrooms, each with its own bath, while the master suite is on the other side for maximum privacy. Amenities in the master suite include a private, fireplace-warmed sitting room and twin walk-in closets on the way to a lavish full bath. A centrally located laundry room on the second floor is an added bonus in this thoughtfully designed home. This home is designed with a basement foundation.

ABOVE: Banks of windows illuminate the interior of this congenial family home. Mutiple dormers and heavy trim molding add character and scale to the pleasing facade.

Plan Number 32512	
Price Code	L
Total Finished	4,056 sq. ft.
First Finished	1,912 sq. ft.
Second Finished	2,144 sq. ft.
Dimensions	61'x63'
Foundation	Basement
Bedrooms	4
Full Baths	4
Half Baths	1

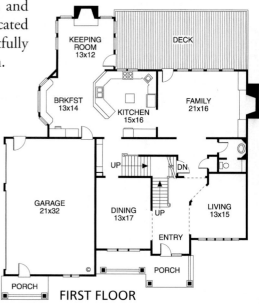

SECOND FLOOR

FIRST FLOOR

Photography: Donna & Ron Kolb, Exposure Unlimited

Spacious and
Gracious

ABOVE: The juxtapositions of angles and arches, and stucco and
stone are unified with heavily detailed white trim to create an
engaging facade for this spacious home.

An arched entry invites you into the interior of this home where elegant window styles and dramatic ceiling treatments create an impressive showcase around a great deal of living space and practicality. Abundant counter space wraps the kitchen, which has easy access to the breakfast area and dining room. The breakfast area opens up to the central great room, with a fireplace flanked by built-ins, high slope ceiling, and elegant arrangement of windows. An extravagant master suite and a bay-front library complete the living space on the main floor. Two secondary bedrooms on the lower level share a full bath. The lower level also offers a large media room with access to a rear patio, a billiard room, an exercise room, and plenty of basement storage. This home is designed with a basement foundation.

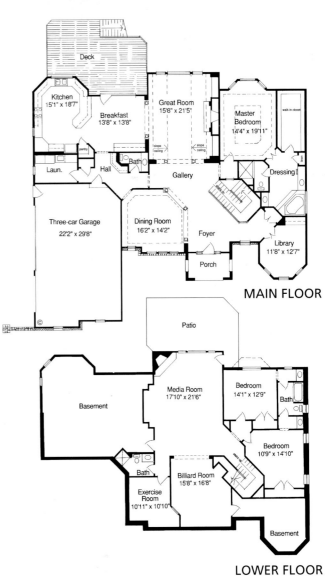

MAIN FLOOR

LOWER FLOOR

Plan Number 92657

Price Code	L
Total Finished	4,328 sq. ft.
Main Finished	2,582 sq. ft.
Lower Finished	1,746 sq. ft.
Basement Unfinished	871 sq. ft.
Deck Unfinished	1,074 sq. ft.
Porch Unfinished	80 sq. ft.
Dimensions	70'8"x64'4"
Foundation	Basement
Bedrooms	3
Full Baths	2
3/4 Baths	1
Half Baths	1

See thousands more plans at www.familyhomeplans.com

Traditional 133

Space for
Every
Purpose

As a private retreat from the busy world, this luxurious home has few peers. The design is well zoned with clearly defined public and private spaces. The dramatic foyer sets the tone for the magnificent home with its balconied overlook and sweeping views. From the entry point, the road leads many ways: to the master suite; to the upstairs bedrooms and bonus room; to the dining room, home office, breakfast area; or to the two-story library. You can even go straight, right out through the French doors onto one of the home's three covered porches. The home is designed with a basement foundation.

ABOVE: Elegant and impressive, this home provides a full range of luxurious space offering a retreat from the busy world.

BELOW: The formal dining room offers plenty of natural light and elegant detailing in the trim and molding. Across the foyer—note the wonderful details of the stunning entry with fan and sidelights—is the equally elegant library.

ABOVE: The arched three-point island frames the work area of the kitchen.

BELOW: The family room opens through French doors to one of the home's three covered porches.

Plan Number 60136

Price Code	L
Total Finished	4,418 sq. ft.
First Finished	3,197 sq. ft.
Second Finished	1,221 sq. ft.
Bonus Unfinished	656 sq. ft.
Basement Unfinished	3,197 sq. ft.
Garage Unfinished	537 sq. ft.
Dimensions	76'x73'10"
Foundation	Basement
Bedrooms	4
Full Baths	3
Half Baths	1

ABOVE: From the front door, the foyer and entry hall look straight through the house to the backyard and pool. To the right is the staircase and the left is the dining room.

FIRST FLOOR

SECOND FLOOR

Traditional 135

Amenities & **Options**

The large foyer, with its elegant open staircase, opens straight ahead through a wide arch spanning the entrance to the formal living and dining rooms. To the left, a smaller hallway leads to a bedroom suite and private den. The right side of the first floor is reserved for the more casual and utilitarian areas. An arched entrance leads you into the kitchen, which shares one large open space with the window-lined breakfast nook and family room. Another arched entrance brings you to a small hall with two closets and access to the laundry room and three-car garage. On the second floor, a long hallway connects the secondary bedrooms and the master suite. Art niches are something to see in between. The master suite is impressive with a large bedroom, exercise room, multiple closets, and five-piece bath. An optional door in one of the closets offers access to an optional second mechanical room. This home is designed with a basement foundation.

ABOVE: Three gabled peaks rising on the front of the facade of the main living area draw attention to the impressive symmetry balancing the wide front porch. A discrete side-load garage keeps the focus on the home's entry.

BELOW: A large arched doorway framed with columns opens the big combination dining and living room to the front hall.

Photography courtesy of the Designer

ABOVE: A peek under the arch into the living room reveals an elegant fireplace with brick surround and a band of tall windows.

LEFT: Windows high above the front door and staircase landing illuminate the foyer, while a built-in plant ledge adds scenery.

Plan Number 97361

Price Code	L
Total Finished	4,448 sq. ft.
First Finished	2,823 sq. ft.
Second Finished	1,625 sq. ft.
Garage Unfinished	959 sq. ft.
Dimensions	85'8"x68'4"
Foundation	Basement
Bedrooms	4
Full Baths	1
3/4 Baths	2
Half Baths	1

SECOND FLOOR

FIRST FLOOR

Photography Mike Moreland

Refined **Comfort**

This home represents a subtle blending of American traditional design and up-to-the-minute creature comforts. With its roots in the classic country estate, the open floor plan provides the versatility of use and ease of movement necessary for modern lifestyles. At 5,288 square feet, it has both the specialized spaces as well as the private and shared spaces a busy family needs today. Elegant proportions and careful design make it all work. Inside the foyer, visitors are ushered straight ahead into the two-story living room, which features a fireplace flanked by built-ins. A perpendicular hallway cuts across the home, connecting the main private space—the master suite—from the shared areas of the home. The spacious master suite visually connects to a well-appointed bath by a see-through fireplace. Another fireplace warms the nearby study. Two sets of stairs lead from the 3,322-square-foot first level to the 1,966-square-foot second level, one stairway curving upward gracefully from the foyer, the other, a more informal stairway, leading up from the opening that connects the living room to the kitchen area. Three bedrooms and three full baths share the upstairs—the farthest bedroom is a suite. This home is designed with a basement foundation.

ABOVE: The stone-clad main gable nicely contrasts with the wood trim and stucco siding on the front elevation.

BELOW: Deep wood tones, crossing box-beams, and a wide fireplace, flanked by arched built-ins, round out the appeal of the private study.

ABOVE: The deck off the living room, looking toward the floor-to-ceiling windows that line the breakfast nook, offers a quiet retreat for casual outdoor dining.

LEFT: Light-filled and elegant, the living room is a rich combination of soaring heights and delicate detailing.

BELOW LEFT: The comfortable family room features a fireplace surrounded by built-ins and a wall of windows.

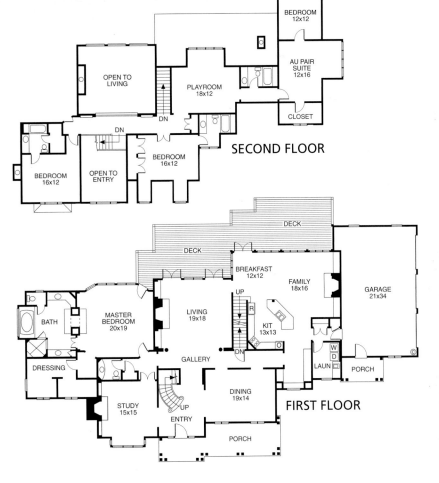

SECOND FLOOR

FIRST FLOOR

Plan Number 32006

Price Code	L
Total Finished	5,288 sq. ft.
First Finished	3,322 sq. ft.
Second Finished	1,966 sq. ft.
Basement Unfinished	3,275 sq. ft.
Garage Unfinished	774 sq. ft.
Deck Unfinished	1,476 sq. ft.
Porch Unfinished	338 sq. ft.
Dimensions	111'2"x66'2"
Foundation	Basement
Bedrooms	4
Full Baths	4
Half Baths	1

ABOVE: Multiple covered porches, varying roof lines, and classic trim details give this house the appearance of a lovely, established home that's been added onto with great care and attention over successive generations. A mix of siding materials adds to the appeal.

Spacious Executive
Home

This spacious plan provides everything a family could need and then some. The public spaces form the core of the home where a two-story entry leads through columns into the two-story great room. To the right, the casual family spaces include a large kitchen that's open to the windowed breakfast area as well as the long keeping room. Also on this side of the home is the service area, which includes a deep walk-in pantry, laundry room, office with private entry, and three-car garage. The master suite shares the left wing with a guest suite and private study. Three more bedrooms can be found on the second floor along with three full baths, a media room, and attic storage. This home is designed with a basement foundation.

SECOND FLOOR

FIRST FLOOR

Plan Number 32368

Price Code	L
Total Finished	6,150 sq. ft.
First Finished	4,136 sq. ft.
Second Finished	2,014 sq. ft.
Basement Unfinished	4,136 sq. ft.
Garage Unfinished	852 sq. ft.
Deck Unfinished	234 sq. ft.
Porch Unfinished	686 sq. ft.
Dimensions	124'9"x64'8"
Foundation	Basement
Bedrooms	5
Full Baths	4
3/4 Baths	1
Half Baths	2

Order on-line at www.familyhomeplans.com

Elegant &
Inviting

ABOVE: A sturdy brick facade is enlivened with bright white paint on elegant trim details. A curved porch roof supported by double columns draws attention to the entry, right where it should be.

BELOW: The covered porch at the rear of the home is a gracious outdoor room perfect for entertaining or relaxing. A door from the family room in close proximity to the kitchen makes it equally ideal for outdoor dining.

Attention to detail is clearly evident throughout this fine home, from the front facade, right through the lovely interior, and out to the gracious covered porch at the rear of the home. A mix of elegantly detailed public and private spaces highlight the first floor. The fine attention to detail caries over even into the utilitarian spaces. A kitchen pantry and a butler's pantry add to the convenience and practicality of the home. Three secondary bedrooms, each with a private bath, share the second floor with a computer loft. This home is designed with a basement foundation.

ABOVE: A series of French doors along the rear wall of the living room lets in the light and opens the room to a big covered porch at the rear of the home. Gloss white trim, a coffered ceiling, and repeated arches above the built-ins and French doors offer understated elegance.

RIGHT: The two-story family room is open to the kitchen and breakfast bay. The stone fireplace surround with thick, natural wood mantel lends a casual charm to this bright and open space.

BELOW: The sweeping curve of the main staircase in the two-story entry makes a lovely first impression.

ABOVE: The master bedroom is a spacious, bright, and open retreat thanks in part to a generous amount of tall windows.

RIGHT: The secluded study at the front of the home.

BELOW: The breakfast nook provides a bright and cheery spot to start the day.

SECOND FLOOR

FIRST FLOOR

Plan Number 32367

Price Code	L
Total Finished	6,526 sq. ft.
First Finished	3,323 sq. ft.
Second Finished	1,625 sq. ft.
Lower Finished	1,578 sq. ft.
Basement Unfinished	1,745 sq. ft.
Garage Unfinished	864 sq. ft.
Porch Unfinished	539 sq. ft.
Dimensions	110'x92'11
Foundation	Basement
Bedrooms	4
Full Baths	4
Half Baths	1

Romantic Revival

In the early 1900s, as the suburb began its gradual dominance over the city as the residential area of choice, the old architectural standbys, charming and attractive as they are, simply weren't right for everyone. Some homebuyers turned to the more fanciful styles of the European countryside—adding, of course, their own Americanized flourishes.

Our collection of Romantic Revival updates features rich detailing and luxurious appointments from red-tiled roofs and elaborate fireplace mantels to rich wood floors and elegant ceiling treatments. Whether a sprawling Mediterranean villa or a charming French country cottage, these picturesque homes offer the modern family the luxury of Old World romance with the convenience of New World amenities.

ABOVE: Curved, copper-top dormers set into a richly tiled roof, Normandy-style windows inside a courtyard wall, and a decorative iron-work gate create a charming front facade.

BELOW: 12-foot high ceilings and 8-foot tall patio doors topped with transoms give a large-scale feel to the moderately sized dining room.

European *Charm*

The courtyard entry, high-profile roofline, and arched French dormers create a slightly deceptive facade. Although it appears to be a large, one and a half-story home, a step through the gracious front door into the open living areas reveals a one-story design that's less than 2,600 square feet. Clever strategies give the moderately sized rooms a big feel. Ceilings in the living and dining rooms soar to great heights. Patio doors in each room are topped by transoms. The kitchen layout is equally suited for meal preparation for two or for large parties, when the island can serve as a buffet and gathering spot. Every wall in the nearby family room has a function: two walls filled with windows provide views into the backyard; a third wall holds built-ins. The master bedroom is separated from the secondary bedrooms and includes patio doors that open to the veranda. This home is designed with a slab foundation.

ABOVE: In the living room, patio doors on exterior-mounted tracks slide open to create clean openings onto the veranda.

RIGHT: French doors lead from the breakfast room to the long rear veranda. A niche in one wall frees floor space.

BELOW: Maple cabinets in the kitchen take on the look of built-in furniture, with varying heights and depths and crown molding.

ABOVE: The master bedroom features ten-foot ceilings and access to the rear veranda. Details in the room such as the built-up crown molding and operable plantation shutters contribute to the Old World charm found throughout the design.

Plan Number 32380

Price Code	D
Total Finished	2,581 sq. ft.
Main Finished	2,581 sq. ft.
Garage Unfinished	602 sq. ft.
Veranda Unfinished	422 sq. ft.
Dimensions	62'x87'8"
Foundation	Slab
Bedrooms	3
Full Baths	2
Half Baths	1

ABOVE: Two walls of tall windows, arched built-ins for the entertainment center, and an open arrangement with the kitchen and breakfast nook contribute to the spacious feel of the family room.

BELOW: A veranda along the back of the home overlooks the pool. Sliding doors open the home to the outdoor space. The doors to the left of the photo lead into the living room while the doors to the right lead into the master bedroom.

MAIN FLOOR

FAMILY
15x18

KIT
12x12

BREAKFAST

BEDROOM
12x12

VERANDA

DINING
13x12

BEDROOM
13x11

LIVING
13x13

UTIL
W D

STUDY
12x11

MASTER
BEDROOM
16x13

ENTRY

GARAGE
27x21

CLOS

BATH

Not Your Average
Country Cottage

ABOVE: This storybook cottage rolls out the welcome mat with a walled courtyard and a three-car garage disguised with shuttered windows.

This plan proves that new homes can have the same well-worn character and quaint features as older homes. Natural materials and French country details give it a time-honored appeal that suits its wooded surroundings. A courtyard, which begs for gardens and a fountain, ushers visitors to the entry. Twelve-foot ceilings in the entry and great room create an airy feeling amid the home's more cozy and defined spaces. To one side of the entry is the dining room with a vaulted ceiling. A private study is on the other side of the hall. The great room, with its proximity to the entry and kitchen, is ideal for entertaining. The kitchen includes an island with seating at one end and a walk-in pantry. It joins the breakfast nook, which has direct access to the great room and three-season porch. A deck beyond the porch provides more outdoor living space. The owners of this home finished off the porch as a sunroom for year-round enjoyment.

The master suite is set into a private corner on the first floor. The adjoining bath features two vanities and a walk-in closet. Completing the 2,079-square-foot first floor are a mudroom and laundry area off the garage that includes a built-in bench and lockers for storing kids' backpacks, coats, and boots.

The secondary bedrooms and a full bath complete the 796-square-foot second floor. Two of the bedrooms have dormers that would make charming areas for children. This home is designed with a basement foundation.

ABOVE: A transom and sidelights framing the front door flood the foyer with light.

RIGHT: This is no ordinary vaulted ceiling in the great room, blending a touch of rococo charm with a classical ogee soffit of subtle curves.

BELOW: The accumulation of details like the wrought-iron courtyard gate, matching lanterns, and segmental brick arch over the doorway add to the charm of the entry.

ABOVE: The nook has French doors opening onto the three-season porch and floor-to-ceiling windows on the adjacent walls.

RIGHT: The vaulted three-season porch allows year-round enjoyment of your property and offers a relaxing retreat at the rear of the home.

BELOW: The multifunctional island not only provides additional workspace, but also an intimate place for casual meals.

ABOVE: The bay window in the master bedroom provides a sunny sitting area.

ABOVE RIGHT: The luxuriously appointed master bath features a coffered ceiling.

RIGHT: Rows of tall windows open up the rear elevation.

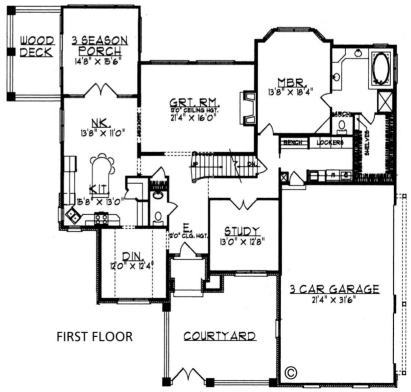

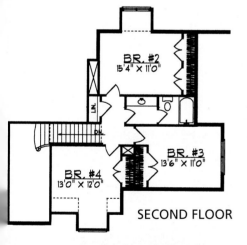

SECOND FLOOR

BR. #2
15'4" X 11'0"

BR. #3
13'6" X 11'0"

BR. #4
13'0" X 12'0"

LIN.

FIRST FLOOR

WOOD DECK

3 SEASON PORCH
14'8" X 15'6"

NK.
13'8" X 11'0"

GRT. RM.
12'0" CEILING HGT.
21'4" X 16'0"

MBR.
13'8" X 18'4"

BENCH   LOCKERS

ARCH

SHELVES

KIT.
15'8" X 13'0"

DIN.
12'0" X 12'4"

E.
12'0" CLG. HGT.

STUDY
13'0" X 12'8"

3 CAR GARAGE
21'4" X 31'6"

COURTYARD

Plan Number 97313

Price Code	G
Total Finished	2,875 sq. ft.
First Finished	2,079 sq. ft.
Second Finished	796 sq. ft.
Porch Unfinished	234 sq. ft.
Dimensions	63'x68'
Foundation	Basement
Bedrooms	4
Full Baths	2
Half Baths	1

*This plan is not to be built within a 100-mile radius of Cedar Rapids, IA.

Spacious and *Comfortable*

This French country manor is roomy, comfortable, and made for enjoying life. With a vaulted ceiling that reaches a height of nearly 18 feet, the lofty great room greets visitors as they enter through the small but elegant porch and foyer. Flanking a stone fireplace with a simple country mantle are two lovely built-ins.

A theme that begins on the exterior with the gentle curve above the den window is refined inside the home. Curves continue throughout the house. At each end of the great room, thick-walled arched openings lead off to the kitchen and to the master suite.

Each room has its curves. The wide entry to the master bedroom is topped off by an elegant, wide curve. We also see the structure of the home in the master bedroom, which shows off its rafters as they rise to the peak of the gabled room.

A similar curved opening leads to the dining room. Outside, the same radius transfers to the three garage doors and the side entry

that leads to the home's mudroom.

In the right wing of the home, in addition to the master bedroom, sitting room, and master bath, there's also a den, all just off a short hall on the right side of the home.

The powder room is next to the garage on the more public left side of the home. On this side is the dining room, great room, kitchen, eating nook, mudroom, garage, and shop. This home is designed with a crawlspace foundation.

ABOVE: A glimpse through the arch peeks into the master bedroom.

LEFT: The tall, vaulted space of the great room.

BELOW: Custom cabinetry in the kitchen.

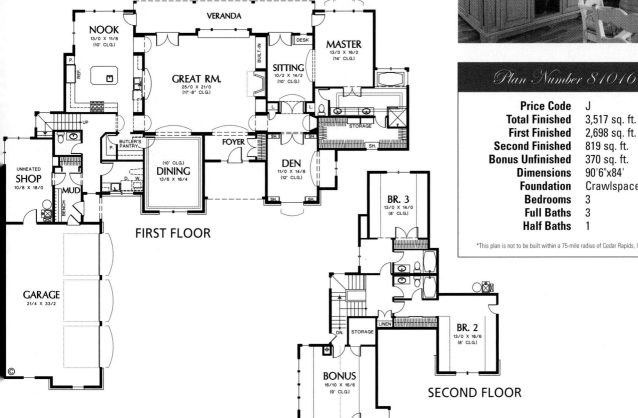

FIRST FLOOR

VERANDA

NOOK
13/0 X 11/8
(10' CLG.)

MASTER
13/0 X 16/2
(14' CLG.)

DESK

BUILT-IN

SITTING
10/2 X 14/2
(10' CLG.)

GREAT RM.
25/0 X 21/0
(17'-8" CLG.)

STORAGE

UP

BUTLER'S
PANTRY

FOYER

UNHEATED
SHOP
10/8 X 18/0

MUD

BENCH

DINING
13/6 X 16/4
(10' CLG.)

DEN
11/0 X 14/8
(12' CLG.)

GARAGE
21/4 X 33/2

SECOND FLOOR

BR. 3
13/0 X 14/0
(8' CLG.)

BR. 2
13/0 X 16/6
(8' CLG.)

DN.

STORAGE

LINEN

BONUS
16/10 X 16/6
(9' CLG.)

Plan Number 81016

Price Code	J
Total Finished	3,517 sq. ft.
First Finished	2,698 sq. ft.
Second Finished	819 sq. ft.
Bonus Unfinished	370 sq. ft.
Dimensions	90'6"x84'
Foundation	Crawlspace
Bedrooms	3
Full Baths	3
Half Baths	1

*This plan is not to be built within a 75-mile radius of Cedar Rapids, Iowa.

Traditional
French Charm

Live large. That's the message the designer of this classic French traditional wanted to express through the home's subtle lines and luxurious details. Probably no room in the house speaks more clearly of leisurely home enjoyment than the great room. With its impressive, window-filled rear wall, this great room lives up to its name. A classic mantle, curved backboard with raised-panels, curved crown molding and gentle carvings and luxurious surround, including display built-ins with hidden storage below, combine to make the fireplace integral to the room's overall impact. The great room dominates the first level and makes an impact even on the upstairs,

which gets flooded with natural light thanks to the window wall.

Also upstairs are three secondary bedrooms, two that share a full bath and a third that comes with its own full bath, walk-in closet and large study area. A curved balcony, open to the foyer on one side and the great room on the other, connects the two sides of the upper floor.

Downstairs, the master suite includes an octagonal space off a corner of the master bath that holds the whirlpool tub. And above the tub, a cathedral ceiling.

Elsewhere you'll enjoy the generous proportions of the den, the dining room with stepped ceiling, the gourmet kitchen with breakfast nook and walk-in pantry, and the

ABOVE: Shallow curves and classic angles merge to form a modern example of classic French country design.

BELOW: The big great room window juts gently into the backyard from the rear facade.

four-car garage that leads into the home through the laundry and mudroom.

Surely not even the French ever expressed the French country lifestyle with more flair. This home is designed with a crawlspace foundation.

Plan Number 93182

Price Code	J
Total Finished	3,517 sq. ft.
First Finished	2,698 sq. ft.
Second Finished	819 sq. ft.
Bonus Unfinished	370 sq. ft.
Dimensions	90'6"x84'
Foundation	Crawlspace
Bedrooms	3
Full Baths	3
Half Baths	1

LEFT: What a great room! A three-sided wall of windows that pokes out into the backyard and a graceful French country mantle and surround of display shelves and built-in storage grace this remarkable space.

BELOW LEFT: The front den is fitted out with dark-toned built-ins to accommodate a home office. The curves of the built-ins echo in the curved entryway to the office, with its glass-paneled, curve-top doors.

BELOW: Drenched in wood and sleek finishes, this gourmet kitchen possesses an almost sculptural quality. Fine woodwork and an efficient layout combine beauty with practicality.

FIRST FLOOR

SECOND FLOOR

Mediterranean *Ease*

At 3,656 square feet, this classic design offers not just the quantity of space you need but the quality of space you expect. Beginning on the 2,329-square-foot first floor, we find a series of exquisite shared spaces, from the two-story living room with French doors leading onto a rear sun deck, to the large kitchen, breakfast nook and keeping room. The master suite takes up the right side of the first floor and incorporates a refined sitting area. Wraparound windows add to the spacious feeling of the area. On the second floor, three secondary bedrooms share two full baths. Adding to the comfort and usefulness of this children's suite is the children's den, which overlooks the two-story living room. This home is designed with a basement foundation.

Order on-line at www.familyhomeplans.com

Price Code	J
Total Finished	3,656 sq. ft.
First Finished	2,329 sq. ft.
Second Finished	1,259 sq. ft.
Lower Finished	68 sq. ft.
Bonus Unfinished	420 sq. ft.
Basement Unfinished	1,806 sq. ft.
Garage Unfinished	528 sq. ft.
Dimensions	77'x66'
Foundation	Basement
Bedrooms	4
Full Baths	2
3/4 Baths	1
Half Baths	1

RIGHT: Light-filled and towering, the two-story living room is anchored around a simple fireplace flanked by dramatic windows.

BELOW: Inside the soaring two-story foyer, stairs lead to the children's domain upstairs. The doorway to the left opens to the two-story living room; the doorway to the right leads to the wing of the home that's devoted entirely to the master suite.

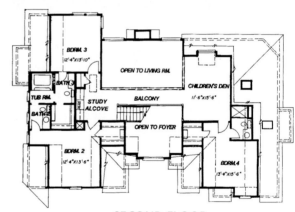

SECOND FLOOR

FIRST FLOOR

A Beautiful
Balancing Act

This French country-inspired design provides space for entertaining and for quiet family time. Floor-to-ceiling windows across the back wall of the living room offer a view from the foyer, right through an open hallway, back to the porch and yard.

Separated from the formal rooms by a solid wall and a short hallway, the family gathering rooms, anchored by a large kitchen, open to one another in great-room style. Rows of transom-topped windows flood the rooms with sunlight. An eating peninsula separates the kitchen from the family room, creating a spectator spot for visitors to chat with the chef. The center island is large enough to hold an optional second sink. Four windows that stretch nearly the full height of the wall light the eating nook. To the left, a doorway to the covered porch makes it easy to keep an eye on dinner cooking on the grill. Nearby, in the family room, one wall is filled with windows—also topped with transoms—while the fireplace is set into an interior wall. There's plenty of room for built-ins to flank the fireplace, providing storage for all the electronic gear a family room requires.

The first-floor master suite faces the backyard and includes a sitting area. The master bath includes a dressing room with dual walk-in closets and a large corner tub lit by glass block windows. An additional first floor bedroom with private bath could serve as a guest room.

The second floor contains two bedrooms but is designed to expand as the family grows. The game room can serve as another bedroom, study, or workout room. The bonus space over the garage could also be an additional bedroom. This house is designed with basement and crawlspace foundation options.

OPPOSITE AND ABOVE: This storybook cottage rolls out the welcome mat with a walled courtyard and a three-car garage disguised with shuttered windows.

RIGHT: Columns detailed with classic moldings and trim visually support arched openings between the dining room and the two-story foyer. The homeowner added some custom touches to this plan including changing a large coat closet next to the main entry into a powder room.

BELOW: The turret is the dominant visual feature on the home's exterior, which includes a covered porch and rear patio near the family room. This modified version of the home was built without the master sitting area and the dormers over the living room that appear on the plan as shown on page 161.

ABOVE LEFT: The big family room is filled with amenities from the fireplace to the wall of windows to the built-in cabinets and entertainment center.

ABOVE: The kitchen is the anchor of the trio of casual family spaces at the rear of the home, which include the family room and a big, sunny breakfast area. Replacing the angled eating bar shown on the floor plan with a center island opens up the space even more.

LEFT: The dining room, steps away from the kitchen yet worlds away from the casual family spaces it lies near, is the epitome of French country elegance.

BELOW: With its open design leading to the bay window breakfast area, the kitchen resembles an old-fashioned galley. The French-country cabinets are custom made and stained a honey brown.

Plan Number 96603

Price Code	L
Total Finished	3,667 sq. ft.
First Finished	2,654 sq. ft.
Second Finished	1,013 sq. ft.
Dimensions	75'4"x74'2"
Foundation	Basement
	Crawlspace
Bedrooms	4
Full Baths	3
Half Baths	1

ABOVE: The master bedroom features eleven-foot ceilings and a sitting area tucked into a rear-projecting bay.

RIGHT: Arched niches in the master bath house twin vanities.

FIRST FLOOR

SECOND FLOOR

Every Room a *View*

This home opens to nature wherever you look. The design of this home steps out of its own footprint to incorporate a separate guest house and enclosed area, which could include a swimming pool, garden, fountain, or serve as a preserve for a large tree or two. The front door that leads you into the home drops you into a dramatic space. Look up from the foyer and you have a spectacular view of the grand salon, a two-story octagon with a triptych of amazingly tall windows. To the left of the grand salon is the master suite, carefully separated from the public areas of the home. Elsewhere, two more rooms are dedicated as bedrooms, both upstairs along with a full bath. The guest house at the front of the home includes a full bath, large walk-in closet, and French doors onto the colonnade. Spacious public rooms in addition to the grand salon include the leisure room, which is open to the kitchen and bay windowed breakfast nook, and a formal dining room, connected to the grand salon, which leads out onto a covered lanai. This home is designed with a slab foundation. Alternate foundation options are available at an additional charge. Please call 1-800-235-5700 for more information.

ABOVE: Looking over the pool through the courtyard, we see the leisure room to the left, the guest house to the right, and the portico entry in the center.

BELOW: A two-story colonnade leads past the courtyard and pool to the home's main entry.

ABOVE: Great lines define this home, with a facade that centers on an inviting entry portico.

RIGHT: The big, open casual spaces surrounding the well-planned kitchen area include a breakfast bay and leisure room.

BELOW: The shapes of the grand salon, accented by high, arched windows, create a room as uniquely beautiful as its view.

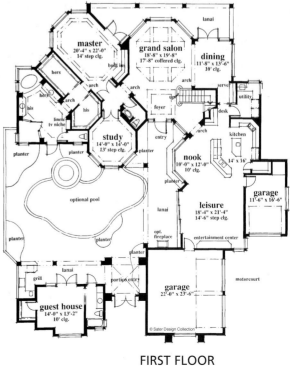

Plan Number 94246

Price Code	K
Total Finished	3,792 sq. ft.
First Finished	2,853 sq. ft.
Second Finished	627 sq. ft.
Guest House Finished	312 sq. ft.
Garage Unfinished	777 sq. ft.
Deck Unfinished	540 sq. ft.
Porch Unfinished	326 sq. ft.
Dimensions	80'x96'
Foundation	Slab
Bedrooms	4
Full Baths	3
Half Baths	1

SECOND FLOOR

FIRST FLOOR

Continental **Manor**

Modeled after the great homes of Europe, this home's exterior only hints at the impressive spaces inside, where ceilings soar to 10 feet on the first floor and 9 feet on the second. French doors are crowned by transoms to give proper proportion to the grand spaces. Unlike many floor plans in which the family room serves as the home's hub, this family room has its own defined space. The breakfast room and screen porch flank the kitchen and add informal space, but do not flow directly into the family room. Separate fireplaces warm the dining room, living room, family room, master suite, and guest bedroom on the 2,936-square-foot first floor. A second-floor library also has a fireplace and adjoins a cozy study. Three secondary bedrooms round out the 1,521-square-foot second floor. The bonus room adds an additional 314 square feet. This home is designed with a basement foundation.

ABOVE: A hip roof, stucco finish, and tall casement windows form a simple, elegant design.

BELOW: Set back from the entry, the gallery, showcasing the open staircase, serves as a buffer between the master suite and living areas.

ABOVE: A stately entrance welcomes visitors to the living room. Heavy crown molding emphasizes the height of the ten-foot ceilings.

BELOW LEFT: The elegant formal dining room, with one of the home's five fireplaces, includes three built-in closets perfect for china, silver, and table linens.

BELOW RIGHT: Built-in bookshelves beside the family room fireplace offer ample space to store—or show off—favorite books and artifacts.

ABOVE: The elegant rear facade mimics the symmetry of the front and is just as attractive. The huge family room enjoys a panoramic view of the backyard, while twin porches extend living space outdoors.

LEFT: With its brick floor, screen walls, and high ceiling, stepping out onto this lovely screen porch is like stepping into a vacation.

SECOND FLOOR

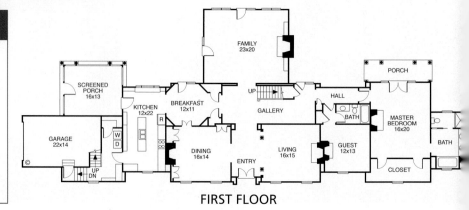

FIRST FLOOR

Plan Number 32033

Price Code	L
Total Finished	4,457 sq. ft.
First Finished	2,936 sq. ft.
Second Finished	1,521 sq. ft.
Bonus Unfinished	314 sq. ft.
Basement Unfinished	2,248 sq. ft.
Garage Unfinished	308 sq. ft.
Dimensions	125'x52'
Foundation	Basement
Bedrooms	5
Full Baths	4

Modern Country Manor

From the tall French doors that open the formal rooms to the front terrace to the balcony off the master bedroom, everything about this home speaks of elegant living. At the rear of the home, a large great room opens to a rear terrace that is also accessible from the first floor guest room. A large kitchen at the center of the family spaces opens to a keeping room that has a covered porch. On the second floor, the master suite is entered through a big sitting room—with fireplace—that also leads to the equally big master bath. There are three additional bedrooms on the second floor and a conveniently located laundry room. This home is designed with a basement foundation.

Plan Number 93648	
Price Code	L
Total Finished	5,326 sq. ft.
First Finished	2,702 sq. ft.
Second Finished	2,624 sq. ft.
Dimensions	74'10"x65'9"
Foundation	Basement
Bedrooms	5
Full Baths	3
Half Baths	1

FIRST FLOOR

SECOND FLOOR

ABOVE: Sloping and hipped rooflines, a gable, a turret, and a rounded dormer give this home an air of regality, while its mix of brick and stone siding lends an earthy, organic touch. The interior provides the same mix of casual and elegant spaces.

Plan Number 50063	
Price Code	L
Total Finished	5,377 sq. ft.
Main Finished	2,961 sq. ft.
Lower Finished	2,416 sq. ft.
Basement Unfinished	271 sq. ft.
Garage Unfinished	758 sq. ft.
Dimensions	89'x59'2"
Foundation	Basement
Bedrooms	3
Full Baths	2
Half Baths	2

Royally Comfortable

The first floor of this elegant plan provides all the spaces needed for daily living. A two-sided fireplace creates a warm welcome in the V-shape foyer. To the right, the impressive master suite, with its own octagonal sitting room, shares a wing with a secluded library. To the left are the common areas. Here the counter-lined kitchen easily serves both the dining room and the breakfast area. Fireplaces warm the great room and the hearth room, casting their glow under decorative ceilings. A laundry room and three-car garage round out the floor.

The walk-out lower floor is a home within itself, designed for entertainment with rooms that cater to every pastime from the exercise room to the media room, the gathering room featuring a bar adjacent to the wine cellar, and a billiards room leading out to the patio. This home is designed with a basement foundation.

LOWER FLOOR

MAIN FLOOR

ABOVE: A Georgian roofline and tall windows create special appeal for this impressive mansion-style home.

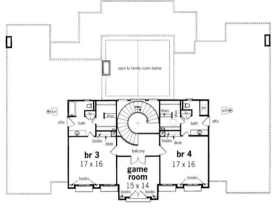

SECOND FLOOR

FIRST FLOOR

Fine *Georgian Flair*

Beside the foyer is a library complete with a trio of built-in bookshelves that's ideal for relaxing with a good book. A two-story ceiling soars above the huge family room, which enjoys the warmth of a fireplace between its built-in bookshelves and entertainment center. Bookshelves and a fireplace enhance the corner den as well. A handy butler's pantry links that kitchen to the front dining room, which includes built-in curio shelves. A central circular staircase winds up to the second floor, where a game room with built-in bookshelves lies between two comfortable secondary bedrooms. This home is designed with slab and crawlspace foundation options.

Plan Number 65665	
Price Code	L
Total Finished	5,560 sq. ft.
First Finished	4,208 sq. ft.
Second Finished	1,352 sq. ft.
Dimensions	94'x68'
Foundation	Crawlspace
	Slab
Bedrooms	4
Full Baths	3
3/4 Baths	1
Half Baths	2

Comfort, Space, and *Amenities*

This showcase Mediterranean-style home was inspired by life on the Mediterranean coast, whether it's in France, Italy, Spain, Greece, or on one of the many islands that dot the ancient blue-green waters of the birthplace of Western culture. This perfect mesh of comfort, space, and amenities features classic lines, open spaces topped by high ceilings, and an ample volume of windows. Inside the main entry, the foyer provides a view out into the great room with its vaulted ceiling. The huge kitchen, breakfast area, and hearth room is a big open-plan space that's perfect for entertaining.

On the main floor, the master suite has a tremendous walk-in closet and capacious bath with step-up tub and discrete shower and water closet. Also on the first floor are a den, home office, formal dining room and two garages—one for two cars and one for a single automobile, boat, or workshop.

The lower floor is where the rest of the family lives. This includes a huge family/recreation room, three bedrooms, an exercise room, lots of storage, and two full baths. This home is designed with a basement foundation.

ABOVE: The long, low lines of a Mediterranean villa are clearly visible in this front elevation taken at dusk.

BELOW: Elegantly tapered Ionic columns support the archways that surround the center hall and separate the entry from the dining room.

ABOVE LEFT: The formal dining area is designed with graceful high ceilings, arched windows, and a niche, which is just the place to set that antique china cabinet.

ABOVE: Built on a hilly site, this home really opens up to the backyard, where raised decks and a screen porch let you enjoy the outdoors.

LEFT: The spacious kitchen, open to the breakfast nook and great room, is at the center of the home.

Plan Number 97315

Price Code	L
Total Finished	5,639 sq. ft.
Main Finished	2,812 sq. ft.
Lower Finished	2,827 sq. ft.
Garage Unfinished	1,136 sq. ft.
Deck Unfinished	113 sq. ft.
Porch Unfinished	182 sq. ft.
Dimensions	95'x62'
Foundation	Basement
Bedrooms	4
Full Baths	3
Half Baths	1

*This home is not to be built within a 75-mile radius of Cedar Rapids, IA.

MAIN FLOOR

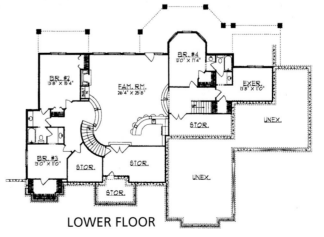

LOWER FLOOR

See thousands more plans at www.familyhomeplans.com

Romantic Revival 171

Shingle Style

Free-form and variable, Shingle style architecture developed in the 1880s as a uniquely American adaptation combining Queen Anne, Colonial Revival, and Richardson Romanesque architectural styles. Wide porches, asymmetrical forms, gambrel roofs, rambling additions, and windows—Palladian windows, bay windows, bands of multiple windows, walls curving into windows—combined to create a picturesque style ideally suited to open, natural settings with spectacular views.

With their emphasis on comfortable, convenient floor plans—informal, open, and spacious with windows opening to the best light and most appealing views—these great Shingle style updates are ideal for today's families, whether as a seasonal vacation home or full-time retreat.

Waterfront Wonder

Cedar shingles and window boxes create a charming front, while numerous windows can offer a splendid view of any scenery. Beside the front entry sits a library with built-in shelving, which connects to a large laundry room. The kitchen's bay window enjoys a built-in banquette, to make casual meals a scenic affair. The dining room is open to the large, fireplace-warmed living room, creating a sense of flow when entertaining, but keeping the warm intimacy for which the home was designed. A hall connects the two second-floor bedrooms to a full bath and a loft nestled into the front center gable. This home is designed with a crawlspace foundation.

ABOVE: Rustic cedar siding, divided-light windows, and a great floor plan cater to year-round lakeside living in this cozy shingle-style home.

Plan Number 32341

Price Code	E
Total Finished	2,282 sq. ft.
First Finished	1,427 sq. ft.
Second Finished	855 sq. ft.
Dimensions	46'6"x35'
Foundation	Crawlspace
Bedrooms	3
Full Baths	2

FIRST FLOOR

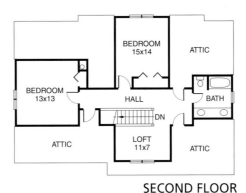

SECOND FLOOR

Proud **Heritage**

Shingle siding and an inviting porch

capture the endless appeal of seaside cottages. A central see-through fireplace adds ambiance to the great room and dining room, both of which enjoy the light and scenery provided by tall windows in rounded bays. The efficient kitchen can serve either the dining room or a breakfast nook with sliding glass doors to a deck in the back corner. Set apart for maximum privacy, the master suite with its walk-in closet and full bath can be found above the two-car garage. Two secondary bedrooms front the second floor, with a hallway connecting them to a balcony above the breakfast room. This home is designed with a basement foundation.

ABOVE: Curves, windows, and outdoor spaces are the themes that define this charming cottage.

Plan Number 32176

Price Code	E
Total Finished	2,390 sq. ft.
First Finished	959 sq. ft.
Second Finished	1,431 sq. ft.
Basement Unfinished	959 sq. ft.
Garage Unfinished	480 sq. ft.
Dimensions	62'x36'
Foundation	Basement
Bedrooms	3
Full Baths	2
Half Baths	1

FIRST FLOOR

SECOND FLOOR

ABOVE: Neutral siding is beautifully set off by the white trim that outlines the screen porch, windows, and arched entry. The Victorian traditions of shingle-style architecture are alive and well in the bays, turrets, gables, and porches of this great design.

BELOW: Large picture windows offer uninterrupted views and fill the interior with light.

New England
Classic

Built for great family times and hearty entertaining, this cottage retreat pays homage to the coastal homes of Maine. The moment guests pass through the barrel-vaulted entry and set foot on the porch, they feel a welcoming presence. The great room is warmed by a corner fireplace and illuminated by floor-to-ceiling windows that provide light from two directions. The deck and screen porch provide places to relax while enjoying outdoor views. Both outdoor spaces have direct access to the eating nook and kitchen.

The master suite, which features another corner fireplace, rounds out the 1,508-square-foot main level. The 947-square-foot upper level features an elevated study surrounded by windows. This level also has two bedrooms with separate baths. A staircase in the garage leads to a large office that can be converted into a suite. This home is designed with a basement foundation.

ABOVE: A window, framed by cabinets and a shelf, brightens up the kitchen. Instead of a peninsula counter, the owners of this home added a central opening that maintains the connection to the living areas while hiding any cooking mess.

LEFT: The brick hearth creates a homey atmosphere in the generous great-room.

BELOW: Informality reigns in the relaxed dining area.

ABOVE: A half-round window in the upstairs study offers water views. The room could be used as a secluded retreat or as fourth bedroom.

ABOVE RIGHT: The large master suite with its fireplace and private access to the rear deck offers a respite from the daily activities of a busy summer on the coast.

RIGHT: The third bedroom also features a half round window. The second floor office—joined to this room by a full bath—is almost as large as the first floor master and could be used as such by parents who want to be close to small children. Then the first floor master would make an ideal study, den, or guest bedroom.

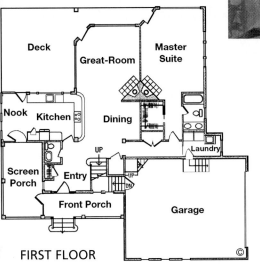

FIRST FLOOR

- Deck
- Great-Room
- Master Suite
- Nook
- Kitchen
- Dining
- Screen Porch
- Entry
- Front Porch
- Garage
- Laundry
- UP

SECOND FLOOR

- Study
- Bedroom 2
- Bedroom 3
- Office

Plan Number 32189	
Price Code	E
Total Finished	2,455 sq. ft.
First Finished	1,508 sq. ft.
Second Finished	947 sq. ft.
Basement Unfinished	1,508 sq. ft.
Garage Unfinished	735 sq. ft.
Dimensions	60'4"x60'
Foundation	Basement
Bedrooms	3
Full Baths	1
3/4 Baths	2
Half Baths	1

Shingle Style

Stylish
Gables

ABOVE: Drawing on Cape Cod influences for a traditional look, the exterior mixes neutral colored shingle siding with crisp white trim to enhance the clean lines of the design. Stepped gables give the home a sense of depth. The rear of the home opens up to the site with abundant windows.

This plan's stylish gables create great curb appeal. A first-floor hall leads past a bedroom and a laundry room to a kitchen with access to a back porch. The nearby dining room conveniently flows into an inviting family room, complete with ample windows and a homey fireplace. A loft overlooks the family room, while connecting three bedrooms. The spacious couple's realm—or master suite—accesses a walk-in closet, a private bath, and a deck over the porch. This home is designed with a basement foundation.

SECOND FLOOR

FIRST FLOOR

Plan Number 32517	
Price Code	F
Total Finished	2,633 sq. ft.
First Finished	1,522 sq. ft.
Second Finished	1,111 sq. ft.
Basement Unfinished	1,512 sq. ft.
Garage Unfinished	543 sq. ft.
Dimensions	41"x86'2"
Foundation	Basement
Bedrooms	4
Full Baths	3

Well
Rounded

A shingled turret spilling onto the porch begins the circular motif that is abundant inside and out. Once inside, columns support an arched canopy-like ceiling, which defines the foyer. A panoramic bank of windows, reminiscent of a ship's bow, occupies a wall in the great room. This rounded design continues in the kitchen, with its gently curved, two-tiered counter. A circular stairway off the foyer leads into the master suite, which occupies the whole upper level. The lower level, also reached via circular stairway, houses the secondary bedrooms. This home is designed with a basement foundation.

ABOVE: This year-round delight blends vintage features with modern spaces in three-levels of living space. More than sixty windows take advantage of the home's waterfront location.

BELOW: The curved library offers excellent acoustics for listening to music.

ABOVE: Birch cabinetry built the same height as the mantel creates the look of wainscoting while providing plenty of storage for electronics.

LEFT: The open plan great room and kitchen are visually separated from the entry by four chunky columns topped by arches that repeat the theme of curves found throughout the home. Just inside the doorway, the stairway climbs the turret to the second floor master suite.

BELOW: The open plan creates a large comfortable space at the core of the home. A curved wall of casement windows beyond the dining table looks out over a side deck.

ABOVE: The home's curves recur throughout the master bath, in the rounded vanity, tub, and circular window. Vertical blinds add privacy when needed.

LEFT: A master suite on the top level takes advantage of the best views. High porthole windows draw light deep into the master bedroom and offers view of sky and stars. Just outside the double entry doors, a balcony overlooks the great room. A curving loft adds architectural interest and a more intimate scale to the voluminous space.

Plan Number 32220

Price Code	F
Total Finished	2,665 sq. ft.
First Finished	1,322 sq. ft.
Second Finished	619 sq. ft.
Lower Finished	724 sq. ft.
Basement Unfinished	483 sq. ft.
Garage Unfinished	440 sq. ft.
Deck Unfinished	232 sq. ft.
Porch Unfinished	187 sq. ft.
Dimensions	76'7"x57'8"
Foundation	Basement
Bedrooms	3
Full Baths	2
Half Baths	1

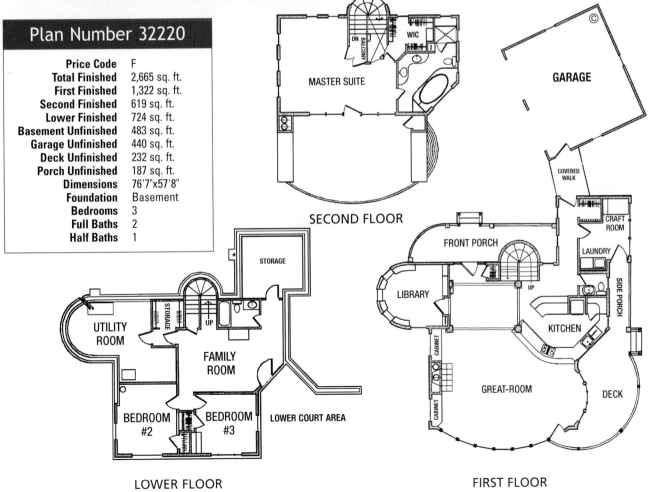

SECOND FLOOR

LOWER FLOOR

FIRST FLOOR

Cape Cod
Flavor

ABOVE: Shingle siding, striking gable shapes, and an angled design bring out the Cape Cod flavor. Oversize gables open up the upper level interior. One bay of the garage has a rear door for a boat.

BELOW: Generously sized windows at the rear of the home soak up the view.

This home is proof that the Cape Cod style is good for any place and any time, not just Cape Cod. With 3,002 square feet of living space, it's even a good deal more versatile than the traditional Cape-style home, as well as beautifully practical with no wasted space. In this plan, the all-purpose family room was deleted in favor of two separate spaces, the living room and dining room. On the upper level, the central staircase purposefully divides bedrooms into an adult side and a children's side. The kitchen is loaded with counterspace and contains a prep zone and easy-to-reach appliances. Above the three-car garage is 400 square feet of bonus space. This home is designed with a crawlspace foundation.

ABOVE: An opening between the house and garage teases arriving guests with a glimpse of the water views to come. Although the garage is detached from the house, the bonus room above the garage connects to the second floor through a short hallway.

BELOW: Framed by an imposing 6-foot-high mantel, the living room fireplace is faced with gray slate. Three sets of French doors lead out onto a rear covered porch.

Shingle Style   183

ABOVE: Semi-custom maple kitchen cabinets wrap a window-lined polygonal work space in the kitchen. French doors in the adjacent breakfast area open the room to the outdoors.

LEFT: The dining room offers great views and casual elegance.

BELOW: The kitchen's upper cabinets are stained dark green. Backsplashes are crafted from the same slate as the living room fireplace surround.

ABOVE: The homeowners modified the master bath layout to showcase their antique clawfoot tub.

LEFT: Evening sunsets can be enjoyed from the private balcony off the master bedroom.

Plan Number 32349

Price Code	H
Total Finished	3,002 sq. ft.
First Finished	1,626 sq. ft.
Second Finished	1,376 sq. ft.
Bonus Unfinished	400 sq. ft.
Garage Unfinished	840 sq. ft.
Porch Unfinished	184 sq. ft.
Dimensions	93'7"x68'6"
Foundation	Crawlspace
Bedrooms	3
Full Baths	2
Half Baths	2

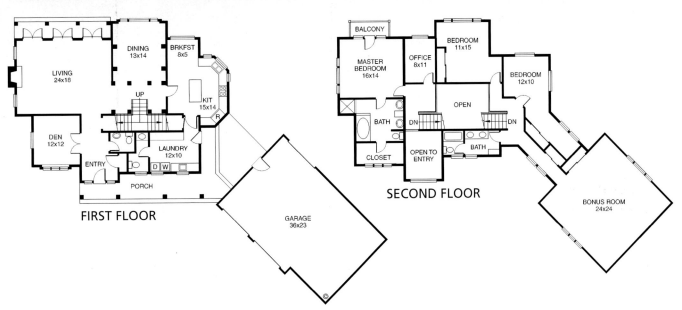

FIRST FLOOR

LIVING 24x18
DINING 13x14
BRKFST 8x5
UP
KIT 15x14
DEN 12x12
LAUNDRY 12x10
ENTRY
PORCH
D W
GARAGE 36x23

SECOND FLOOR

BALCONY
MASTER BEDROOM 16x14
OFFICE 8x11
BEDROOM 11x15
BEDROOM 12x10
OPEN
BATH
DN
DN
CLOSET
OPEN TO ENTRY
BATH
BONUS ROOM 24x24

Shingle Style

Photography: Tommy Miyasaki

Sublime Shingle-Style

The best of old-world styling and modern convenience join in this traditional shingle-sided home. Abundant windows and high ceilings maximize natural light and views, throughout the 2,267-square-foot first floor. The large great room, which reaches out back through a full-width bay window, soars two stories tall and is warmed by a fireplace wall flanked on one side by built-in storage and on the other by a bar. Just off the great room, sheltered by a lowered ceiling, a cozy kitchen is outfitted with a spacious storage island and surrounded by beautiful built-ins. A sunroom and long porch add to the enjoyment of this home. Also downstairs, a secondary bedroom with full bath occupies one end of the home while the master suite is located up front in its own private complex that includes a large bath, walk-in closet, and private study.

The 813-square-foot second floor includes two generously sized bedrooms, a full bath, and a private porch. Those upstairs can enjoy whatever is going on in the great room thanks to windows that look down on the events below. This home is designed with a combination basement/slab foundation.

ABOVE: Traditional shingle siding and elegant low-arch window and door openings provide classic appeal.

BELOW: The morning light brings out the natural golden glow in the home's weather-resistant cedar shingles.

Order on-line at www.familyhomeplans.com

Price Code	H
Total Finished	3,080 sq. ft.
First Finished	2,267 sq. ft.
Second Finished	813 sq. ft.
Basement Unfinished	467 sq. ft.
Garage Unfinished	527 sq. ft.
Dimensions	56'x99'8"
Foundation	Combo Basement/ Slab
Bedrooms	4
Full Baths	3
3/4 Baths	1

LEFT: A wide arched window illuminates the study, which includes a corner fireplace and built-ins.

BELOW LEFT: Just off the great room, the beautiful and well-organized kitchen comes with plenty of storage, including a two-tiered storage peninsula.

BELOW: Secluded on the first floor, the master suite has its own bay window overlooking the rear porch.

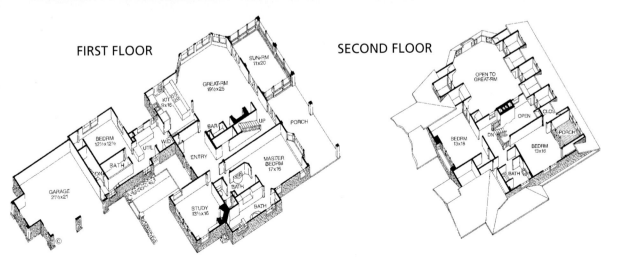

FIRST FLOOR

SECOND FLOOR

Room to **Relax**

ABOVE: Crisp gables and natural materials blend this home with its lush surroundings.

This plan's hub is definitely the open great room, warmed by a fireplace and found at the end of the front entry. French doors open from the great room into a sunporch, while a wall of windows looks onto a more traditional porch on the side. Plentiful counter space accents the kitchen, which easily connects to the breakfast room and a nearby laundry room. A home office in one back corner offers a secluded and private work space. The vaulted bedroom on the upper floor enjoys access to a luxurious full bath and a room-sized walk-in closet, while a second office and a guest room share a full hall bath. The lower-floor garage is big enough to house three cars and offers additional storage space. This home is designed with a basement foundation.

Plan Number 32072

Price Code	I
Total Finished	3,406 sq. ft.
First Finished	1,847 sq. ft.
Second Finished	1,405 sq. ft.
Lower Finished	154 sq. ft.
Basement Unfinished	294 sq. ft.
Garage Unfinished	1,461 sq. ft.
Dimensions	43'6"x52'
Foundation	Basement
Bedrooms	2
Full Baths	2
Half Baths	1

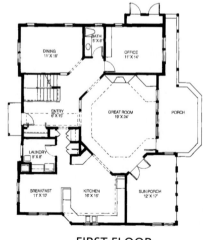

LOWER FLOOR

FIRST FLOOR

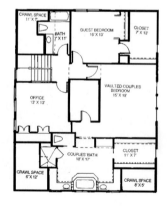

SECOND FLOOR

Photography Beth Singer

ABOVE: From the front, arches, gables, and a recessed window niche work beautifully with the classic shingle siding to create a visual composition of comfort and prosperity.

BELOW: Imagine the views you could enjoy from the cantilevered rear deck, which bows out from the two-story great room.

Glorious Great Room

Although clearly beautifully designed, guests must step inside this home to appreciate its high level of invention. Twin wings flank the home's showpiece: an immense great room that rises two stories tall and includes a curving second-floor gallery that shares its upstairs hallway space with a curved home library. The opposite wing is comprised of the bow-front breakfast area and a large kitchen. To the sides of the entry hall sit a powder room, home office, and formal dining room. Private spaces include the master suite, which features a huge master bedroom with an arched wall of windows, twin walk-in closets and a well-designed bath. A handsomely designed bonus room, with an adjacent full bath, adds 401 square feet. This home is designed with a basement foundation.

ABOVE: French doors in the great room lead onto the curved rear deck, while two stories of windows draw in natural light. The marble hearth holds a gas fireplace.

LEFT: Practicality reigns in the kitchen with a big, convenient layout. The kitchen opens to the bright breakfast bay lined with floor-to-ceiling windows and topped with skylights.

Plan Number 32606

Price Code	I
Total Finished	3,474 sq. ft.
First Finished	2,569 sq. ft.
Second Finished	905 sq. ft.
Bonus Unfinished	401 sq. ft.
Basement Unfinished	2,522 sq. ft.
Garage Unfinished	680 sq. ft.
Dimensions	62'10"x74'7½"
Foundation	Basement
Bedrooms	3
Full Baths	3
Half Baths	1

Order on-line at www.familyhomeplans.com

ABOVE: The curved gallery that overlooks the great room also includes a built-in home library space, which is visible in the curved wall behind the railing.

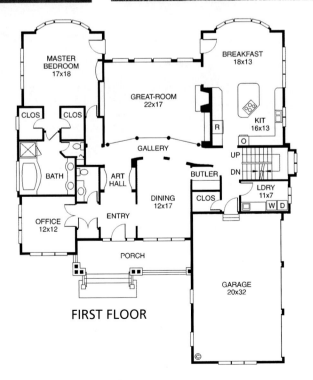

FIRST FLOOR

MASTER BEDROOM 17x18

CLOS

CLOS

GREAT-ROOM 22x17

BREAKFAST 18x13

KIT 16x13

R

O

BATH

GALLERY

UP

DN

ART HALL

BUTLER

LDRY 11x7

W D

CLOS

OFFICE 12x12

ENTRY

DINING 12x17

PORCH

GARAGE 20x32

SECOND FLOOR

OPEN TO GREAT-ROOM

CLOS

CLOS

BEDROOM 13x12

BONUS 13x19

GALLERY

OPEN

LIBRARY

CLOS

DN

OPEN TO ENTRY

BEDROOM 12x15

The Right Stuff

Gables facing toward the street project a welcoming warmth that's typical of traditional cottage design. What's not typical of cottage design is this home's 3,560 square feet of amenity-packed living space.

The front porch, sheltered by a beautifully curved roof, greets visitors. Inside the main entry is the welcoming foyer, where visitors get a view of the formal dining and living rooms. Past the stairs to the second floor, the home opens into a kitchen/breakfast area and family room arrangement that's just the thing for family get-togethers and informal entertaining. On the 2,348-square-foot first floor, the master suite's location promotes privacy. The 1,212-square-foot second floor incorporates two more bedrooms, a loft, and a room designed for all sorts of activities. This home is designed with a crawlspace foundation.

Plan Number 32098

Price Code	J
Total Finished	3,560 sq. ft.
First Finished	2,348 sq. ft.
Second Finished	1,212 sq. ft.
Garage Unfinished	608 sq. ft.
Porch Unfinished	140 sq. ft.
Dimensions	62'4"x82'
Foundation	Crawlspace
Bedrooms	3
Full Baths	2
Half Baths	1

ABOVE AND RIGHT: The big kitchen-breakfast room-family room space at the rear of the home is lined with big windows. Custom cabinets in the kitchen retain the cottage feel.

BELOW RIGHT: A vaulted ceiling with exposed beams in the master bedroom adds a clever, traditional touch to the room.

SECOND FLOOR

FIRST FLOOR

Natural Beauty

Ideal as a vacation home, this plan's mix of comfortable spaces and sensible layout make it practical as a full-time residence too. The front porch opens into a large two-story living room, which forms the core of the home. To one side of the first floor is the master suite, which features a fireplace, walk-in closet, a large tub, and a separate shower. The opposite end of the home contains the kitchen, dining room, and study. A half-circle island and L-shaped cabinet space in the kitchen provide plenty of work space for cooking and entertaining. The dining room is surrounded on three sides by glass that lets occupants survey the backyard. The study is a more private space. The two-story living room divides the 1,471-square-foot second floor, creating the need for two sets of stairs. One staircase rises to two large secondary bedrooms, each with its own private bath. The other staircase leads to a third bedroom, also with its own bath as well as a private covered deck. This home is designed with a basement foundation.

ABOVE: The best elements of Victorian shingle style—from the multiple cross-gables to the bay windows and ample porches—evidence themselves in the facade of this great home.

BELOW: A two-story living room with large hearth proudly displays the handsome rafters and collar ties that keep it strong and secure.

ABOVE: Lots of room with lots of storage are found in this kitchen, which is outfitted for big families or frequent entertaining.

BELOW: This homeowner modified the plan to open up the dining room to the kitchen, creating an open, comfortable space.

ABOVE: A big screen porch at the back of the house adds extra living space for dining, entertaining, or just relaxing.

BELOW: The big first-floor master retains its cottage charm with its own fireplace and the small, shuttered windows centered between the two larger ones.

Plan Number 32378

Price Code	J
Total Finished	3,593 sq. ft.
First Finished	2,122 sq. ft.
Second Finished	1,471 sq. ft.
Basement Unfinished	1,619 sq. ft.
Garage Unfinished	953 sq. ft.
Deck Unfinished	180 sq. ft.
Porch Unfinished	715 sq. ft.
Dimensions	61'x55'
Foundation	Basement
Bedrooms	4
Full Baths	3
3/4 Baths	1
Half Baths	1

FIRST FLOOR   SECOND FLOOR

Wide and Welcoming

With its sturdy plank floor and beadboard ceiling, this home's wide front porch is an outdoor sanctuary that provides a place for children to play on a rainy day or for adults to enjoy the outdoors anytime. Built-in cabinets enhance the wide gallery hall that separates the formal and informal living spaces on the 2,018-square-foot first floor. The two-story great room, with its massive fireplace, dominates the rear of the home. On one end of the great room, French doors open onto a luminous sunroom. All four bedrooms are on the 1,859-square-foot second floor. The main staircase off the gallery hall rises to the balcony hall that leads to the master suite. A secondary staircase near the kitchen ascends to the wing that houses three additional bedrooms and an informal family gathering space. This home is designed with a crawlspace foundation.

ABOVE: Cedar shingles, a wide porch, and irregular, "added-onto" shapes outfit this home in high Shingle-style.

BELOW: A deep wraparound porch with plank flooring and beadboard ceiling easily accommodates a variety of outdoor furnishings, creating an outdoor sanctuary on both fair and rainy days.

RIGHT: A massive fireplace visually dominates the great room. French doors at one end open to the sunroom.

BELOW: The U-shape kitchen is anchored by a long center island.

ABOVE: Removed from the family areas of the home, the formal dining room, which is open to the entry hall, looks out onto the front porch.

RIGHT: A fireplace surrounded by display cabinetry warms the cozy living room.

BELOW: These French doors in the second-level master bedroom lead out onto a private deck that's built over the front porch.

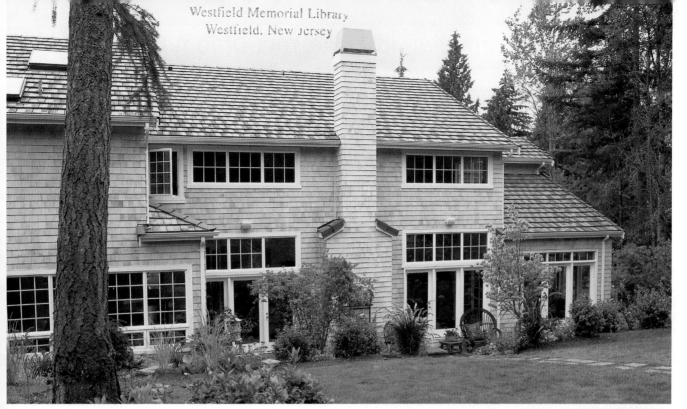

ABOVE: The kitchen, sunroom, and great room all have doors that open to the rear of the home.

RIGHT: Surrounded by windows on two sides, including French doors that lead onto the rear deck, the sunroom is a luminous retreat in all seasons.

SECOND FLOOR

FIRST FLOOR

NOTE: The house as built in these photographs has been reversed from the plan shown on this page.

Plan Number 32114

Price Code	K
Total Finished	3,877 sq. ft.
First Finished	2,018 sq. ft.
Second Finished	1,859 sq. ft.
Garage Unfinished	816 sq. ft.
Deck Unfinished	867 sq. ft.
Dimensions	86'6"x55'
Foundation	Crawlspace
Bedrooms	4
Full Baths	2
Half Baths	1

*This plan is not available for construction in Island, King, Kitsap, Pierce, or Snohomish counties in the state of Washington.

See thousands more plans at www.familyhomeplans.com

Shingle Style 199

Important Information to Make Your Dream Come True

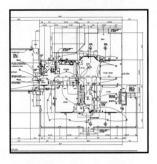

Detailed Floor Plans

The floor plans of your home accurately depict the dimensions of the positioning of all walls, doors, windows, stairs, and permanent fixtures. They will show you the relationship and dimensions of rooms, closets, and traffic patterns. The schematic of the electrical layout may be included in the plan.

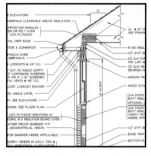

Typical Wall Section

This section will address insulation, roof components, and interior and exterior wall finishes. Your plans will be designed with either 2x4 or 2x6 exterior walls, but if you wish, most professional contractors can easily adapt the plans to the wall thickness you require.

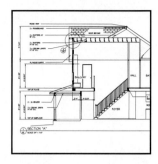

Typical Cross Section

A cut-away cross section through the entire home shows your building contractor the exact correlation of construction components at all levels of the house. It will help to clarify the load bearing points from the roof all the way down to the basement. Available for most plans.

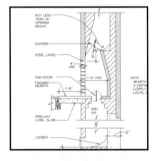

Fireplace Details

If the home you have chosen includes a fireplace, a fireplace detail will show typical methods of constructing the firebox, hearth, and flue chase for masonry units, or a wood frame chase for zero-clearance units. Available for most plans.

Foundation Plan

These plans will accurately show the dimensions of the footprint of your home, including load-bearing points and beam placement if applicable. The foundation style will vary from plan to plan. (Please note: There may be an additional charge for optional foundation plan. Please call for details.)

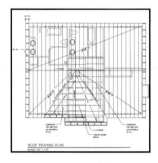

Roof Plan

The information necessary to construct the roof will be included with your home plans. Some plans will reference roof trusses, while many others contain schematic framing plans. These framing plans will indicate the lumber sizes necessary for the rafters and ridgeboards based on the designated roof loads.

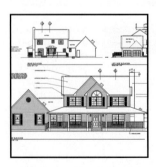

Exterior Elevations

These front, rear, and side views of the home include information pertaining to the exterior finish materials, roof pitches, and exterior height dimensions.

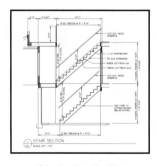

Stair Details

If the design you have chosen includes stairs, the plans will show the information that you need in order to build them—either through a stair cross section or on the floor plans.

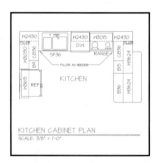

Cabinet Plans

These plans, or in some cases elevations, will detail the layout of the kitchen and bathroom cabinets at a larger scale. Available for most plans.

Garlinghouse Options & Extras

Reversed Plans can Make Your Dream Home Just Right

You could have exactly the home you want by flipping it end-for-end. Simply order your plans "reversed." We'll send you one full set of mirror-image plans (with the writing backwards) as a master guide for you and your builder. The remaining sets of your order will come as shown in this book so the dimensions and specifications are easily read on the job site. Most plans in our collection will come stamped "reversed" so there is no confusion. We can only send reversed plans with multiple-set orders. There is a $50 charge for this service. Some plans in our collection are available in "Right Reading Reverse." Right Reading Reverse plans will show your home in reverse. This easy-to-read format will save you valuable time and money. Please contact our Sales Department at 800-235-5700 to check for Right Reading Reverse availability. There is a $135 charge for this service. **RRR**

Remember to Order Your Materials List

Available at a modest additional charge, the Materials List gives the quantity, dimensions, and specifications for the major materials needed to build your home. You will get faster, more accurate bids from your contractors and building suppliers and avoid paying for unused materials as well as waste. Materials Lists are available for all home plans except as otherwise indicated, but can only be ordered with a set of home plans. Due to differences in regional requirements and homeowner or builder preferences, electrical, plumbing and heating/air conditioning equipment specifications are not designed specifically for each plan. **ML**

What Garlinghouse Offers

Home Plan Blueprint Package

By purchasing a multiple-set package of blueprints or a Vellum from Garlinghouse, you not only receive the physical blueprint documents necessary for construction, but you are also granted a license to build one (and only one) home. You can also make simple modifications, including minor non-structural changes and material substitutions, to our design as long as these changes are made directly on the blueprints purchased from Garlinghouse and no additional copies are made.

Home Plan Vellums

By purchasing Vellums for one of our home plans, you receive the same construction drawings found in the blueprints, but printed on vellum paper. Vellums can be erased and are perfect for making design changes. They are also semi-transparent, making them easy to duplicate. But most importantly, the purchase of home plan Vellums comes with a broader license that allows you to make changes to the design (i.e., create a hand drawn or CAD derivative work), to make copies of the plan, and to build one home from the plan.

License to Build Additional Homes

With the purchase of a blueprint package or Vellums, you automatically receive a license to build one home and only one home. If you want to build more homes than you are licensed to build through your purchase of a plan, then additional licenses must be purchased at reasonable costs from Garlinghouse. Inquire for more information.

Modifying Your Design Easily

How to Modify Your Garlinghouse Home Plan

Simple modifications to your dream home, including minor non-structural changes and material substitutions, can be made by you and your builder with the consent of your local building official, by marking the changes directly on your blueprints. However, if you are considering making significant changes to your chosen design, we recommend that you use the services of The Garlinghouse Design Staff. We will help take your ideas and turn them into a reality, just the way you want.

Here's our procedure:

Call 800-235-5700 and order your modification estimate. The fee for this estimate is $50. We will review your plan changes and provide you with an estimate to draft your specific modifications before you purchase the vellums. **Please note: A vellum must be purchased to modify a home plan design.** After you receive your estimate, if you decide to have Garlinghouse do the changes, the $50 estimate fee will be deducted from the cost of your modifications. If, however, you chose to use a different service, the $50 estimate fee is non-refundable. **(Note: Personal checks cannot be accepted for the estimate.)**

A 75% deposit is required before we begin making the actual modifications to your plans.

Once the design changes have been completed to your vellum plan, a representative will call to inform you that your modified vellum plan is complete and will be shipped as soon as the final payment has been made. For additional information, call us at 1-800-235-5700. Please refer to the Modification Pricing Guide for estimated modification costs.

Reproducible Vellums for Local Modification Ease

If you decide not to use Garlinghouse for your modifications, we recommend that you follow our same procedure of purchasing vellums. You then have the option of using the services of the original designer of the plan, a local professional designer, or an architect to make the modifications.

With a vellum copy of our plans, a design professional can alter the drawings just the way you want, then you can print as many copies of the modified plans as you need to build your house. And, since you have already started with our complete detailed plans, the cost of those expensive professional services will be significantly less than starting from scratch. Refer to the price schedule for vellum costs.

IGNORING COPYRIGHT LAWS CAN BE A $100,000 MISTAKE

What You Can't Do

U.S. copyright laws allow for statutory penalties of up to $100,000 per incident for copyright infringement involving any of the copyrighted plans found in this publication. The law can be confusing. So, for your own protection, take the time to understand what you can and cannot do when it comes to home plans.

You Cannot Duplicate Home Plans

Purchasing a set of blueprints and making additional sets by reproducing the original is illegal. If you need more than one set of a particular home plan, you must purchase them.

You Cannot Copy Any Part of a Home Plan to Create Another

Creating your own plan by copying even part of a home design found in this publication without permission is called "creating a derivative work" and is illegal.

You Cannot Build a Home Without a License

You must have specific permission or a license to build a home from a copyrighted design, even if the finished home has been changed from the original plan. It is illegal to build one of the homes found in this publication without a license.

MODIFICATION PRICING GUIDE

The average prices shown below represent the most commonly requested changes. Prices for changes will vary depending on the number of modifications requested, the house size, quality of original plan, format provided and method of design used by the original designer. Typically, modifications cost around $1500, excluding the price of the (hand-drawn or computer generated) vellum.

Please contact us to get your $50 estimate at: 1-800-235-5700

CATEGORIES	AVERAGE COST
Adding or removing living space (square footage)	Quote required
Adding or removing a garage	Starting at $400
Garage: Front entry to side load or vice versa	Starting at $300
Adding a screened porch	Starting at $280
Adding a bonus room in the attic	Starting at $450
Changing full basement to crawlspace or vice versa	Starting at $220
Changing full basement to slab or vice versa	Starting at $260
Changing exterior building materials	Starting at $200
Changing roof lines	Starting at $360
Adjusting ceiling height	Starting at $280
Adding, moving or removing an exterior opening	$65 per opening
Adding or removing a fireplace	Starting at $90
Modifying a non-bearing wall or room	$65 per room
Changing exterior walls from 2"x4" to 2"x6"	Starting at $200
Redesigning a bathroom or a kitchen	Starting at $120
Reverse plan right reading	Quote required
Adapting plans for local building code requirements	Quote required
Engineering and Architectural stamping and services	Quote required
Adjust plan for handicapped accessibility	Quote required
Interactive Illustrations (choices of exterior materials)	Quote required
Metric conversion of home plan	Starting at $400

How Does Zip Quote Work?

Obtaining a Construction Cost Calculation Based on Labor Rates and Building Material Costs in Your Zip Code Area.

When you call to order, you must choose from the options available for your specific home in order for us to process your order. Once we receive your Zip Quote order, we process your specific home plan building materials list through our Home Cost Calculator which contains up-to-date rates for all residential labor trades and building material costs in your zip code area. The result?

A calculated cost to build your dream home in your zip code area. This calculation will help you (as a consumer or a builder) evaluate your building budget. All database information for our calculations is furnished by Marshall & Swift, L.P. For over 60 years, Marshall & Swift L.P. has been a leading provider of cost data to professionals in all aspects of the construction and remodeling industries.

Itemized Zip Quote

Option 1

The Itemized Zip Quote is a detailed building materials list. Each building materials list line item will separately state the labor cost, material cost, and equipment cost (if applicable) for the use of that building material in the construction process. This building materials list will be summarized by the individual building categories and will have additional columns where you can enter data from your contractor's estimates for a cost comparison between the different suppliers and contractors who will actually quote you their products and services. The price of your Itemized Zip Quote is based upon the pricing schedule of the plan you have selected, in addition to the price of the materials list. Please refer to the pricing schedule on our order form. **An Itemized Zip Quote is available for plans where you see this symbol.** `ZIP`

Bottom-Line Zip Quote

Option 2

The Bottom-Line Zip Quote is a one line summarized total cost for the home plan of your choice. This cost calculation is also based on the labor cost, material cost, and equipment cost (if applicable) within your zip code area. Bottom-Line Zip Quote is available for most plans. Please call for availability. The price of your initial Bottom-Line Zip Quote is $29.95. Each additional Bottom-Line Zip Quote ordered in conjunction with the initial order is only $14.95. A Bottom-Line Zip Quote may be purchased separately and does NOT have to be purchased in conjunction with a home plan order. **A Bottom-Line Zip Quote is available for all plans under 4,000 sq. ft. or where you see this symbol.** `BL`

*Please call for current availability.

The Itemized and Bottom-Line Zip Quotes give you approximated costs for constructing the particular house in your area. These costs are not exact and are only intended to be used as a preliminary estimate to help determine the affordability of a new home and/or as a guide to evaluate the general competitiveness of actual price quotes obtained through local suppliers and contractors. **Land, landscaping, sewer systems, site work, contractor overhead and profit, and other expenses are not included in our building cost figures. Excluding land and landscaping, you may incur an additional 20% to 40% in costs from the original estimate.** Garlinghouse and Marshall & Swift L.P. cannot guarantee any level of data accuracy or correctness in a Zip Quote and disclaim all liability for loss with respect to the same, in excess of the original purchase price of the Zip Quote product. All Zip Quote calculations are based upon the actual blueprints and do not reflect any differences or options that may be shown on the published house renderings, floor plans, or photographs.

CAD Files Now Available

A CAD file is available for plans where you see this symbol.

Cad files are available in .dc5 or .dxf format or .dwg formats (R12, R13, R14, R2000). Please specify the file format at the time of your order. You will receive one bond set along with the CAD file when you place your order. **NOTE: CAD files are NOT returnable and can not be exchanged.**

Detail Plans

Information on Construction Techniques—NOT PLAN SPECIFIC

PLEASE NOTE: The detail plans are not specific to any one home plan and should be used only as a general reference guide.

Because local codes and requirements vary greatly, we recommend that you obtain drawings and bids from licensed contractors to do your mechanical plans. However, if you want to know more about techniques—and deal more confidently with subcontractors—we offer these remarkably useful detail sheets. These detail sheets will aid in your understanding of these technical subjects.

$19.95 per set
(includes postage)

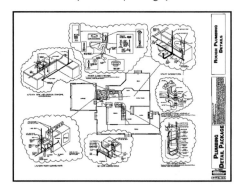

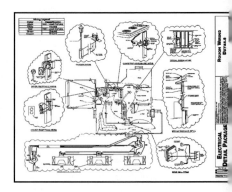

Residential Construction Details

Ten sheets that cover the essentials of stick-built residential home construction. Details foundation options—poured concrete basement, concrete block, or monolithic concrete slab. Shows all aspects of floor, wall and roof framing. Provides details for roof dormers, overhangs, chimneys and skylights. Conforms to requirements of Uniform Building code or BOCA code. Includes a quick index and a glossary of terms.

Residential Plumbing Details

Eight sheets packed with information detailing pipe installation methods, fittings, and sized. Details plumbing hook-ups for toilets, sinks, washers, sump pumps, and septic system construction. Conforms to requirements of National Plumbing code. Color coded with a glossary of terms and quick index.

Residential Electrical Details

Eight sheets that cover all aspects of residential wiring, from simple switch wiring to service entrance connections. Detail distribution panel layout with outlet and switch schematics, circuit breaker and wiring installation methods, and ground fault interrupter specifications. Conforms to requirements of National Electrical Code. Color coded with a glossary of terms.

Your Blueprints Can Be Sealed by A Registered Architect

We can have your home plan blueprints sealed by an architect that is registered in most states. Please call our Order Department for details. Although an architect's seal will not guarantee approval of your home plan blueprints, a seal is sometimes required by your state or local building department in order to get a building permit. Please talk to your local building officials, before you order your blueprints, to determine if a seal is needed in your area. You will need to provide the county and state of your building site when ordering an architect seal on your blueprints, and please allow additional time to process your order (an additional five to fifteen working days, at least). **Seals are available for plans numbered 0-15,999; 17,000-18,999; 20,000 - 31,999; and 34,000 - 34,999.**

State Energy Certificates

A few states require that an energy certificate be prepared for your new home to their specifications before a building permit can be issued. Again, your local building official can tell you if one is required in your state. You will first need to fill out the energy certificate checklist available to you when your order is placed. This list contains questions about type of heating used, siding, windows, location of home, etc. This checklist provides all the information needed to prepare your state energy certificate. **Please note: energy certificates are only available on orders for blueprints with an architect's seal. Certificates are available for plans numbered 0-15,999; 17,000-18,999; 20,000 - 31,999; and 34,000 - 34,999.**

Specifications & Contract Form

We send this form to you free of charge with your home plan order. The form is designed to be filled in by you or your contractor with the exact materials to use in the construction of your new home. Once signed by you and your contractor it will provide you with peace of mind throughout the construction process.

Questions?
**Call our customer service department
1-800-235-5700.**

Order Form

CUSTOMER SERVICE
Questions on existing orders?

1-800-895-3715

To order your plan on-line
using our secure server, visit:
www.familyhomeplans.com

TO PLACE ORDERS
• To order your home plans
• Questions about a plan

1-800-235-5700

Order Code No. **H5BAH**

___ Set(s) of blueprints for plan #_____ $_____

___ Vellum for plan #_____ $_____

___ Foundation _____ $_____

___ Additional set(s) @ $50 each for plan #_____ $_____
(Not available for 1 set-study set)

___ Mirror Image Reverse @ $50 each $_____

___ Right Reading Reverse @ $135 each $_____

___ Materials list for plan #_____ $_____

___ Detail Plans *(Not plan specific)* @ $19.95 each
   ❏ Construction   ❏ Plumbing   ❏ Electrical $_____

___ Bottom-Line Zip Quote @ $29.95 for plan #_____ $_____

___ Additional Bottom-Line Zip Quotes
   @ $14.95 for plan(s) #_____ $_____

Zip code where building _____

___ Itemized Zip Quote for plan(s) #_____ $_____

Shipping $_____

Subtotal $_____

Sales Tax *(VA residents add 4.5%. Not required for other states.)* $_____

TOTAL AMOUNT ENCLOSED $_____

Send your check, money order, or credit card information to:
(No C.O.D.'s Please) *Prices subject to change without notice.*

Please submit all United States & other nations orders to:
The Garlinghouse Company
Attn: Order Fulfillment Dept.
4125 Lafayette Center Drive, Suite 100
Chantilly, VA 20151
CALL: (800) 235-5700   FAX: (703) 222-9705

Credit Card Information
Charge To: ❏ Mastercard   ❏ Visa   ❏ American Express   ❏ Discover

Card # |_|_|_|_|_|_|_|_|_|_|_|_|_|_|_|_|_|_|_|

Signature _____ Exp. ____/____

Please Submit all Canadian plan orders to:
The Garlinghouse Company
102 Ellis Street
Penticton, BC V2A 4L5
CALL: (800) 361-7526   FAX: (250) 493-7526

Payment must be made in U.S. funds. Foreign Mail Orders: Certified bank checks in U.S. funds only

TERMS OF SALE FOR HOME PLANS: All home plans sold through this publication are copyright protected. Reproduction of these home plans, either in whole or in part, including any direct copying and/or preparation of derivative works thereof, for any reason without the prior written permission of Garlinghouse, LLC, is strictly prohibited. The purchase of a set of home plans in no way transfers any copyright or other ownership interest in it to the buyer except for a limited license to use that set of home plans for the construction of one, and only one, dwelling unit. The purchase of additional sets of that home plan at a reduced price from the original set or as a part of a multiple-set package does not entitle the buyer with a license to construct more than one dwelling unit.

Name: _____
Street: _____
City: _____
State: _____ Zip Code: _____
Daytime Phone: _____
Email Address: _____

Privacy Statement (please read)

Dear Valued Garlinghouse Customer,
Your privacy is extremely important to us. We'd like to take a little of your time to explain our privacy policy.
   As a service to you, we would like to provide your name to companies such as the following:
• Building material manufacturers that we are affiliated with, who would like to keep you current with their product line and specials.
• Building material retailers that would like to offer you competitive prices to help you save money.
• Financing companies that would like to offer you competitive mortgage rates.
   In addition, as our valued customer, we would like to send you newsletters to assist in your building experience. We would also appreciate your feedback by filling out a customer service survey aimed to improve our operations.
   You have total control over the use of your contact information. You let us know exactly how you want to be contacted.
(Please check all boxes that apply.)
   ☐ Don't mail
   ☐ Don't call
   ☐ Don't E-mail
   ☐ Only send Garlinghouse newsletters and customer service surveys
   In closing, we hope this shows Garlinghouse's firm commitment to providing superior customer service and protection of your privacy. We thank you for your time and consideration.
Sincerely,
The Garlinghouse Company

Blueprint Order Information

Garlinghouse 2005 Blueprint Price Code Schedule
*Prices subject to change without notice.

Price Code	1 Set Study Set	4 Sets	8 Sets	Vellums	Materials List	Bottom-Line ZIP Quote
A	$395	$435	$485	$600	$60	$29.95
B	$425	$465	$515	$630	$60	$29.95
C	$450	$490	$540	$665	$60	$29.95
D	$490	$530	$580	$705	$60	$29.95
E	$530	$570	$620	$750	$70	$29.95
F	$585	$625	$675	$800	$70	$29.95
G	$630	$670	$720	$850	$70	$29.95
H	$675	$715	$765	$895	$70	$29.95
I	$700	$740	$790	$940	$80	$29.95
J	$740	$780	$830	$980	$80	$29.95
K	$805	$845	$895	$1,020	$80	$29.95
L	$825	$865	$915	$1,055	$80	$29.95

Additional sets with original order $50

Shipping — (Plans 1-35999)	1-3 Sets	4-6 Sets	7+ & Vellums
Standard Delivery (UPS 2-Day)	$25.00	$30.00	$35.00
Overnight Delivery	$35.00	$40.00	$45.00

Shipping — (Plans 36000-99999)	1-3 Sets	4-6 Sets	7+ & Vellums
Ground Delivery (7-10 Days)	$15.00	$20.00	$25.00
Express Delivery (3-5 Days)	$20.00	$25.00	$30.00

International Shipping & Handling	1-3 Sets	4-6 Sets	7+ & Vellur
Regular Delivery Canada (10-14 Days)	$30.00	$35.00	$40.00
Express Delivery Canada (7-10 Days)	$60.00	$70.00	$80.00
Overseas Delivery Airmail (3-4 Weeks)	$50.00	$60.00	$65.00

For Our USA Customers:
Order Toll Free: 1-800-235-5700
Mon.- Fri. 8:00 a.m. - 8:00 p.m. EST.
Sat. 10:00 a.m. - 4:00 p.m. EST.
or FAX your Credit Card order to 1-703-222-9705
All foreign residents (except Canada) call 1-703-547-4154

TO PLACE ORDERS
• To order your home plans
• Questions about a plan
1-800-235-5700

CUSTOMER SERVICE
Questions on existing orders?
1-800-895-3715

For Our Canadian Customers:
Order Toll Free: 1-800-361-7526
Mon.-Fri. 8:00 a.m. to 5:00 p.m. PST.
or FAX your Credit Card order to 1-250-493-7526
Customer Service: 1-250-493-0942

Please have ready: 1. Your credit card number 2. The plan number 3. The order code number **H5BAH**

Before ordering, please read all ordering information.

How Many Sets of Plans Will You Need?
The Standard 8-Set Construction Package
Our experience shows that you'll speed up every step of construction and avoid costly building errors by ordering enough sets to go around. Each tradesperson wants a set—the general contractor and all sub-contractors: foundation, electrical, plumbing, heating/air conditioning, and framers. Don't forget your lending institution, building department, and, of course, a set for yourself. * Recommended For Construction *

The Minimum 4-Set Construction Package
If you're comfortable with arduous follow-up, this package can save you a few dollars by giving you the option of passing down plan sets as work progresses. You might have enough copies to go around if work goes exactly as scheduled and no plans are lost or damaged by sub-contractors. But for only $60 more, the 8-set package eliminates these worries. * Recommended For Bidding *

The 1 Set-Study Set
We offer this set so you can study the blueprints to plan your dream home in detail. They are stamped "study set only—not for construction" and you cannot build a home from them. In pursuant to copyright laws, it is illegal to reproduce any blueprint. 1 set-study sets cannot be ordered in a reversed format.

To Reorder, Call 800-235-5700
If you find after your initial purchase that you require additional sets of plans, a materials list, or other items, you may purchase them from us at special reorder prices (please call for pricing details) provided that you reorder within six months of your original order date. There is a $28 reorder processing fee that is charged on all reorders. For more information on reordering plans, please contact our Sales Department.

An Important Note About Building Code Requirements
All plans are drawn to conform to one or more of the industry's major national building standards. However, due to the variety of local building regulations, your plan may need to be modified to comply with local requirements—snow loads, energy loads, seismic zones, etc. Do check them fully and consult your local building officials. A few states require that all building plans used be drawn by an architect registered in that state. While having your plans reviewed and stamped by such an architect may be prudent, laws requiring non-conforming plans like ours to be completely redrawn forces you to unnecessarily pay very

large fees. If your state has such a law, we strongly recommend yo contact your state representative to protest. The rendering, floor plan and technical information contained within this publication are no guaranteed to be totally accurate. Consequently, no information from this publication should be used either as a guide to constructing home or for estimating the cost of building a home. Complet blueprints must be purchased for such purposes.

Customer Service/Exchanges Call 800-895-3715
If for some reason you have a question about your existing order, pleas call 800-895-3715. Your plans are custom printed especially for you onc you place your order. For that reason we cannot accept any returns. for some reason you find that the plan you have purchased from does not meet your needs, then you may exchange that plan for an other plan in our collection. We allow you 60 days from your origin invoice date to make an exchange. At the time of the exchange, yo will be charged a processing fee of 20% of the total amount of yo original order, plus the difference in price between the plans (if app cable), plus the cost to ship the new plans to you. Call our Custom Service Department for more information. Please Note: Reproducib Vellums can only be exchanged if they are unopened.

Important Shipping Information
Please refer to the shipping charts on the order form for service avc ability for your specific plan number. Our delivery service must have street address or Rural Route Box number—never a post office bc (PLEASE NOTE: Supplying a P.O. Box number will only will delay th shipping of your order.) Use a work address if no one is home during th day. Orders being shipped to APO or FPO must go via First Class Mc Please include the proper postage. For our International Custome only Certified bank checks and money orders are accepted and mu be payable in U.S. currency. For speed, we ship international orders Parcel Post. Please refer to the chart for the correct shipping cost.

Important Canadian Shipping Information
To our friends in Canada, we have a plan design affiliate in Penticto BC. This relationship will help you avoid the delays and charg associated with shipments from the United States. Moreover, c affiliate is familiar with the building requirements in your commun and country. We prefer payments in U.S. currency. Please call c Canadian office at toll free 1-800-361-7526 for current Canadian pric